1916 — 1918

A
WAR DIARY

The Naval & Military Press Ltd

Published by

The Naval & Military Press Ltd
Unit 5 Riverside, Brambleside
Bellbrook Industrial Estate
Uckfield, East Sussex
TN22 1QQ England

Tel: +44 (0)1825 749494

www.naval-military-press.com
www.nmarchive.com

In reprinting in facsimile from the original, any imperfections are inevitably reproduced and the quality may fall short of modern type and cartographic standards.

MAAIKENSHOF
BEDFORD HILLS, NEW YORK

June 12th, 1922.

The author of this diary, a true diary of peace, once remarked, "small as the army was before the war, I wonder at its size"; written from this point of view, the book is a vivid picture of personal experience during three years of war.

Lieutenant H. M. Adams, 2/8th, Battalion Worcester Regiment, was christened "George" by his most intimate friends in France,- a fact he does not record in the following pages; but, when it is added to the above quotation, it may have some significance to the reader.

This diary may hold special interest for members of the Field family, both present and future, since "George" was my best friend during those trying days of 1916 and 1917.

We served together in the 183rd Brigade from the 21st of July 1916 to the 14th of February 1918, and in the same unit,- the 183rd Light Trench Mortar Battery, from the 6th of September 1916 to the 5th of November 1917. During those fourteen months we shared our joys and tribulations, and today I feel that "George" is perhaps the best friend I have.

Harry Field

A WAR DIARY

PREFACE

THIS diary has been printed partly in response to the suggestions of one or two friends who have seen it, and whose names appear in its pages, and partly for my own gratification. Except that a few details have been added from Army notebooks and letters, it remains practically as it was first written, generally in instalments, three to four weeks after the events occurred. It is, and aims at being, little more than a plain record of daily personal happenings, and was written in the first place without any idea of its ever being printed, but rather as a means of informing my family at the time what I was doing, more fully than was possible in letters, and also of acting as a framework upon which my memory in after days could hang and co-ordinate the smaller and externally unimportant details of that time, interesting to the individual but to no one else : and it is as a framework for the reader's details that it may possibly be of some interest to anyone else but myself. After this it is almost needless to disarm criticism beforehand by saying that the diary lays no claim to literary or artistic merit, and is unblushingly egotistical from start to finish. Lastly, it is possible that some may find themselves in their judgment unduly criticised here. Of these I would ask pardon, and would suggest to them that a cool and judicial mind was not always at command in those days, and that the war is now—even officially—at an end.

H. M. ADAMS.

To make anything one writes . . . public, is giving everybody leave under one's own hand to call one fool.—H. WALPOLE to H. S. Conway, 24 July, 1746.

You see, it is simply a very young *man's* record of *his* own thoughts and impressions, and consequently meant for publication.—OSCAR WILDE. Importance of being Earnest (slightly altered).

WAR DIARY

Wednesday, May 24th, 1916.
   We breakfasted at 6.0 a.m. alfresco by the side of the C.O.'s house, Candahar Barracks, Tidworth, as all the mess furniture had been removed. Parade at 7.20 a.m., laden with everything we possessed. I was carrying my pack, full to overflowing, and two haversacks, the equipment one and another, one on each side. A fire had been lighted close to the B Company parade ground to burn up rubbish, and incidently a small quantity of rifle ammunition, which kept popping off at intervals. The roll was called, and I found myself, for perhaps the first and only time, in front of the full strength of my platoon—some sixty men—and all laden as heavily as myself. Everyone seemed very cheery. We entrained at Tidworth Station at 9.0 a.m., and were greeted by the 3/7th Worcesters in camp on Perham Down as we passed. We reached Southampton at 11.0 a.m. and sat about in a goods shed for an hour or two. I had a bet with Symons as to whose equipment was heavier, and lost by a few ounces, on the station scales. We were presently moved off to the dock side into a big shed, passing the Aquitania on the way, lying alongside. It was very hot in the shed, and some of the men went to sleep. I went out and had some fruit at a small restaurant near by and also posted a letter. At 6.45 p.m. we embarked on a smallish mail boat and immediately put on cork or thistledown lifebelts. At 9.0 we pushed off down Southampton Water and the Solent, passing some amazingly powerful searchlights in forts, apparently in mid-channel, though it was too dark to see anything. All the officers and nearly all the men went below. I found it too stuffy and tried to go to sleep on a seat on deck. About midnight it began to rain and became fairly cold.

Thursday, 25th May.
   We reached Havre at 4.30 a.m. and berthed, lying alongside till 7.30, when we disembarked. I managed to get a shave and a bit of a wash on board before we disembarked. We marched round the docks a little way and formed up on a railway siding where we saw some German prisoners engaged in pushing trucks, under French supervision. After a short rest we marched through the town, where the civilians would insist

on passing between the platoons of a company and so break the column, and then up a terrific hill in baking heat to No. 1 Rest Camp, some four miles away. We got up without dropping a man, which we were told was unusual, though I daresay they tell some sort of story to everyone. In the camp we were given tents and left to our own devices. I took Pte. Burford, Rowe's servant, with me, and talking my first French since 1914 bought some bread, sardines, fruit, and vin ordinaire.

At 3.30 p.m. we fell in again and marched down the hill, this time to a large goods yard where the men were told off in 40's to their respective cattle-trucks in an enormously long train. We, the officers, had some ordinary 3rd class corridors, six in a compartment, which with the kit we were all carrying did not leave too much spare room. We had some more food before starting, and the men bought coffee at a stall presided over by two English women. We started at 7 p m.—the longest train I ever was in, containing the whole battalion and transport; less D Company, left behind in the Rest Camp.

Friday, 26th May.
Not much sleep last night. I managed to get a corner seat at breakfast time, and kept it the rest of the way. We stopped at Abbeville at 7.30 a.m. for an hour. The train never seems to go much more than twenty miles an hour, and the men sit in the doorways of their trucks with their feet hanging out—rather a strange sight to see all down the train. At the halts we get out and walk up the train to see how they are getting on—some 200 yards away, and then as the train starts so slowly we can comfortably get in when our compartment comes past. We came up the coast route by Etaples, Boulogne, and Calais, almost getting in sight of England again. At Calais we turned south through St. Omer and had rather a thrilling moment when we first came on to our 1:100000 maps just past Calais. No one knew where we were going. Somebody suggested Ypres, but the point was decided when, just beyond St. Omer, we turned south through Aire to Berguette. From the train we saw an aeroplane with some white balls of shrapnel smoke near it ! At Berguette we all got out, and I, as billeting officer, rode on with orders from the Staff Captain and a guide to Robecq. Here we were met by an interpreter who had arranged all the billets, making everything very simple. The battalion came along about 7.0 p.m., very tired, as I was. No. 8 platoon, my platoon, were in two barns, one at an estaminet where I slept, the other a little way down the road—both quite comfortable. I had a little brick paved bedroom with a bed and sheets on a straw mattress—a luxury I did not expect.

Saturday, 27th May.
I had to get up at 6.0 a.m. to meet D Company who were supposed to come then, but did not actually arrive till the afternoon. During last night we had heard the guns and seen flashes in the sky ; but for all that this place is wonderfully peaceful. While waiting for this company I bought a tin of pears and ate them, sitting on a heap of stones by the road side. Presently a man came out of a house near by and asked me to go in and sit down, which I did, and drank some coffee he offered me. Then

his son appeared, on six days' leave from the front, and we talked for some time. I gave up D company and returned to the mess which Rabone runs very well, though for drink we have to have wine or soda with ' Grenadine,' some red stuff which I don't like much. All the water has to be chlorinated or boiled. The rest of the morning I spent struggling about shewing the Colonel where everything was and trying to keep awake meanwhile. I slept on my bed during part of the afternoon and also censored No. 8's letters, which I find a very lengthy business. I also wrote one letter for Pte. F. Green, who can neither read nor write. Major Griffiths came to dinner in the company mess and we had quite a good spread. Bed about 10.30.

Sunday, 28th May.
We had a short march this morning. The men do not seem able to march very well here, and nor can I, for some reason. The weather is very hot and stifling and the country almost on sea level. After lunch all officers went over to the Hotel de Ville, St. Venant, where we were spoken to by General Haking. He was very genial and even amusing and welcomed us to the XIth corps. He said he had seen us at the King's inspection the other day at Bulford and liked the look of us. He also said he should come and see us whenever we came out of the line, but I have never seen him since that day. We came back and I sat in a little orchard behind my billet writing while the men bathed in a stagnant ditch one field further on. I also had an ' altogether ' wash there later in the evening.
The company at this date consisted of Capt. Cliff, from Evesham ; Capt. Rowe, Worcester ; Lieut. Rabone, Birmingham ; Lieut. Ball, Torquay, come to us with the rest of the draft from the 4th Devons ; then myself and A. F. Franklin, from near Bredon, Second Lieuts.

Monday, 29th May.
Nothing much to do. The men seem very happy in their barns. The chief difficulty is water. None of the numerous ditches round here may be used, and really no one would care to use them, for they stink horribly. There is an almost stagnant stream at the end of the field behind my billet where the men bathe and where I went and washed this afternoon.

Tuesday, 30th May.
We had a very quiet morning, but in the afternoon marched to St. Venant and were inspected as a brigade (183rd) by XIth Corps and 1st Army, the latter being General Munro. While they were going round and we were standing stiffly to attention one of the 1st Army Staff A.D.C.'s touched me on the shoulder and whispered that he hadn't seen me for years. At first I could not think who he was, but then remembered it was Troutbeck, who used to play Corelli trios in Langley's rooms at the House.
In the evening there was a good deal of gunfire to the east—somewhere by Neuve Chapelle. We learnt afterwards that it was a German raid on the Notts. and Derbys in the 35th (Bantam) Division.

CROIX BARBEE

Wednesday, 31st May.

We spent the morning cleaning up billets and in the afternoon moved to La Fosse, a few miles nearer the line. It was frightfully hot and the brigade missed the way. We marched round aimlessly a long way and Edge fell off his horse into the ditch, which I am sorry to say I did not see : a little amusement would have been more than welcome. After a ten mile round we reached our billets. This place, La Fosse, smells more than I could have believed it possible. My billet is not so good as the last one. For one thing, you can only get to the bedroom through the estaminet ; and the bed I don't trust, and so sleep in my fleabag on a ground sheet. I rode over in the afternoon on a bicycle to Hinges for some money from the Field Cashier, who gave me a little kind of cheque book on which I may draw 125 francs three times a month.

Thursday, 1st June.

Spent most of the day in inspections of various kinds—gas-helmets, rifles, kit, &c. In the evening (as we are too close up to move by day) we went forward once more, by platoons this time, to Croix Barbée. B company is now attached for instructions to the 15th Cheshires, a battalion of 'Bantams' in the 35th Division. I and No. 8 went to Z company, billetted in a deserted farm on the road running N.E. from the Croix Barbée cross roads. They seem a very nice lot of people and have an excellent mess, much better than ours. When I arrived I found two men making a bed for me out of rabbit wire stretched on a wooden frame. The houses here are almost all damaged in some way, and a few quite destroyed. The Company Commander, Capt. Morgan, known as Daddy, is young but very efficient. His second in command, Capt. Le Mesurier, is equally efficient and amusing. There is here also a doctor, padre, and a subaltern, Cunningham by name.

Friday, 2nd June.

Breakfast about nine. I am more or less a free lance, and can go where I like and see what I like. I went up with L.-Cpl. Lucas as my orderly to "B Lines," where we had a working party, and from there Cunningham—alias Nuncle—took me up to the front line, passing through the Chateau garden to the north of and adjoining Neuve Chapelle village. The front line consisted of a double wall of sandbags about seven feet high, the space between the walls being the trench. Behind all was open but out of view if one kept close up to the sandbags. I looked through a periscope but could not see much but two belts of brown wire, ours and the Germans'. I saw Symons up there with A company, who are 'in' now. Two or three shrapnel shells came over to the left which annoyed one of the officers in the line very much. He said he was sure they were meant for the battalion on the left and thought the Bosch gunner must have forgotten to chalk his cue this morning. There are many little wooden crosses about near B lines. Near one cross roads I saw three graves : the first "To a British soldier in loving memory," the second "to two German soldiers R.I.P.," and the third "to a French civilian."

In the afternoon I had a hot bath at Croix Barbée, where they have installed boilers to bathe 50 men in an hour.

Saturday, 3rd June.
Quiet day. At 4 p.m. I was told to report at Bn. Hq. for a gas course. I had hoped we had finished with courses in England. I went up half way to the line taking Pte. Halford to Hq. and was told to go to La Fosse. On the way back we were treated to some spent aeroplane shrapnel, some bits coming down within ten yards or so. From the Cheshires' billet I walked to La Fosse, where I was told the course was 'off.' However I had my valise and put up for the night with Bomford, the Quartermaster, and J. L. Bomford, who was going on the course with me.

Sunday, 4th June.
Breakfast and lunch at La Fosse. Bomford and I decided not to hurry back, especially as he has to go back to the line to-night. We got back to our forward billets by tea time. There was a good deal of strafing in the night, down towards Richebourg, they said; anyhow not opposite here.

Monday, 5th June.
In the morning I obtained permission to go round the " posts," isolated defensive points behind the main front line system. I took Pte. Halford again and went round by Loretto and Euston. Just as we reached the La Bassée road from Euston Post they put a shrapnel shell on to the orchard across the road. It rather startled us for the moment as we heard the bullets go ripping through the leaves of the trees. On the way back over the emergency road the nose cap of an Archie fell quite close to us with a whizz like a real shell, which I thought it was until it landed.

In the afternoon they put a fair amount of shrapnel over the batteries in front without doing any damage.

Tuesday, 6th June.
Wet day. I went up to the front line this morning and saw Symons and Evers. The former was half buried last night with a "rum-jar" which took the skin off his fingers, killed two men, and wounded his servant.

Nothing on in the afternoon.

Wednesday and Thursday, 7th and 8th June.
Nothing of interest to record. I went to the front line again Thursday.

Friday, 9th June.
Made preparations in the morning to go up the line. The padre held a short service for the company, a few prayers and a couple of hymns, rather nice, I thought. We got in before dark, the left hand company of the battalion on the left of 'Chateau Road,' and have excellent unstrafed trenches to look after. During the afternoon and evening everything was curiously silent. At 10 p.m. our guns began to flatten the Huns opposite the Gloucesters on our right. The Huns wasted no time in replying and sent over some very heavy stuff like timed heavy H.E.—the Cheshires called it aerial torpedoes. Very little came our way, though the noise was pretty terrific and we kept close to the parapet. Their machine guns were wonderful, ripping along just above our parapet. About midnight the Gloucesters went over and raided the Bosch very

successfully, capturing two machine guns. Things quieted down by about 2.0 a.m. and we got some sleep. I have a minute dugout about 6 feet by 4 by 3 into which I can just crawl with my equipment. There are plenty of mice about.

Saturday, 10th June.
Quite a quiet day in contrast to last night. That however was a good introduction for our men, who took it very well, being quite cheery all the time.

Whit Sunday, 11th June.
We had to clear out at 9.0 a.m., leaving the Cheshires, which I was very sorry to do, as they are such pleasant people, and run their company so very well. We marched by platoons to Riez Bailleul. Some mistake had been made here, as we found the 4th Gloucesters in possession, and some of the men, I believe, had to sleep out. I was told to go up into the line with an N.C.O. to take over from the Welsh Bantams the brigade on the left of the Cheshires. Battalion again made a mistake, sending up all platoon commanders instead of one per company, so there was no room for us when we arrived. We struggled up South Tilleloy trench for nearly two miles turning and twisting round traverses and all on rather slippery duckboards. I took up Cpl. Knight with me, but did not see much of him up there. Ball, Franklin, and myself wandered about and were shewn a few things. The trenches are bad compared with our late ones, as there are a lot of mines just here, and the earth, or rather blue clay, is brought up in sandbags and stacked all about making a great mess. The mines are full of water which has to be constantly pumped out.

Monday, 12th June.
We struggled back to Riez Bailleul after the morning " stand to " and had an omelette at an estaminet. Then about a mile up the road I found company headquarters, lay down on a stone floor and slept till 4 p.m. We could not start back to go in till dark, about 9.0 p.m., and it took us about two and a half hours to get to the front line. No. 8 is in a support trench, about fifty yards behind the front line, and rather better built, though it gets enfiladed by rifle fire from the left at night.

Tuesday, 13th June.
It began to rain early this morning and went on all day. We began preparations for one or two new dugouts in my support line, as accommodation is very limited. The smell here is pretty bad. One 'site' had to be abandoned as they came across an English officer in full kit. There are only too many such just round here, and quantities of wooden crosses to 'one' or 'two unknown British soldiers.' I went down the Duck's Bill sap in A company's frontage and into the crater at the end, reputed to be the largest on the front. It is sixty or seventy yards across, with a pool of water in the middle. There are three other craters on our frontage known as the Colvin craters. The middle and largest one is nearly as big as the Duck's Bill. We hold the far side with a listening post—not very jovial work as the Germans have a sap coming to within fifteen yards of our post.

Wednesday, 14th June.
Rain all night and all to-day. The place is becoming disgusting, what with the smells and the mud : and it is rather cold too. I have to share a noisome little den with Ball and Rabone, and no one is allowed inside a dugout at night.

Thursday, 15th June.
Suddenly about 1 a.m. a machine gun opened up and instantly the whole line on both sides for about a mile took it up, machine guns and rapid rifle fire all going as fast as possible. This pandemonium went on for about half an hour and then died away. No one knew how or why it began. I came off duty at 4.30 a.m. and slept till 9.30 a.m., which was rather good.

Franklin went sick to-day with 'trench feet.' He was frost bitten in Canada : so Ball and I have to get along by ourselves. It is under these conditions that one would welcome a mine going up or something of the kind, to take our minds off the rain.

Friday, 16th June.
The rain stopped this morning about 11 o'clock : everything is sodden and horrid. We spent the day in feverish anticipation of our relief. This began by the arrival of the Gloucesters at 10 p.m. We moved off at midnight. All went well as far as Rue Du Bacquerot, at the bottom end of South Tilleloy, where by bad luck we halted for a moment. A stray bullet coming over at a range of at least 3,500 yards hit my Cpl. Knight at the back of the neck. He did not seem to be much hurt, and drove off down the La Bassée road in an ambulance which I got from near Euston Post. The company moved on, Capt. Cliff and I in rear so tired that we rolled from side to side of the road as though we were drunken. We reached Riez Bailleul at 3.0 a.m.

Saturday, 17th June.
Ball and I had not apparently slept very long when a masked figure burst into the room and announced a gas attack. It was one of the company sergeants. We got up and went outside, but could not smell anything. We walked quietly down the road with our helmets in our hands, occasionally getting a whiff of chlorine, until we met Rowe and several others standing heavily masked. They took them off when we came up, and sniffed suspiciously, and decided it was safe. Apparently it blew down from Armentières. We moved back again this morning to Croix Barbée, the Cheshires billets, though B company is on the cross roads, quite a good house, and not too much knocked about. I spent the afternoon in having a bath and in searching the countryside successfully for a bed.

Sunday, 18th June.
A voluntary church parade (they wanted a compulsory one in full view of the Bosche balloons) was held this morning in front of an 18-pounder battery position, and in view of three observation balloons. About 200 men attended. The result of this was that between 1 and 2 p.m. the Bosche put over about 30 5.9's close to the battery and C company's billet, and made a jolly mess of the road.

Monday, 19th June.

I went to see No. 8 holding Loretto post, taking Weeks, my servant, with me. I gave them some of the photos I took in the trenches at Bedlam buildings, Tidworth. In the afternoon I went with Major Griffiths to the Q.M. stores on the road to La Fosse to look at some bully beef tins recently dug up out of a ditch. It appeared to be all right, and so will be used. In fact we had some ourselves. I had another bath.

Tuesday, 20th June.

Breakfast at 8. Took a working party up to B lines. The men were carried off by an R.E. officer, and I saw little more of them. I met Bigwood of the 7th Worcesters up there. His company are holding B lines, and they gave me a very good lunch. Afterwards I went some way along B lines looking for 'souvenirs.' It was the old Hun support line before March, 1915, and all their dugouts were still to be seen—smashed in. Our men were engaged in clearing them out, and found several Hun water bottles and pieces of equipment. At 2 p.m. I told the R.E. I thought we had had enough. He agreed, and I took the men away

Wednesday, 21st June.

The battalion moved back to La Fosse. I went on independently with 50 men, mostly No. 8, to Lestrem, as a working party, reporting to O.C. Roads, XIth Corps. I fell in with a very nice interpreter who found billets for me and the men; and we settled in. I mess with the O.C. Roads—a very nice captain, and one or two other miscellaneous A.S.C. or R.E. people. My billet is a good one, with a bed and sheets.

Thursday, 22nd June.

Parade at 8.0 a.m., and began work on the light railway, loading road material, stone, &c., into waggons to put on the roads near Croix Barbée. I had breakfast about 9, and then went back and watched the men. There was really nothing in the world I could do, and at one o'clock we knocked off, as no more waggons appeared. During the afternoon I sat in my billet and read.

Friday, 23rd June.

Same programme as yesterday varied by one or two thunderstorms and pretty heavy rain. In the afternoon I found a suitable shop and had a hair cut and very delightful shave. From my bedroom window I did a sketch of the river Lawe, which marks the high water mark of the German advance in 1914, though the church on this side the river has been pretty heavily shelled. After dinner in the mess we went into the church, which is quite handsome. I asked the curé if anyone was allowed to play the organ, but he said they only played it on festivals; though I could play the little one if I liked. This turned out to be an old harmonium inside the altar rails.

Saturday, 24th June.

Very nice day, though rather hot. Work in the morning as before, and another shave in the shop, as my razor is broken. Sitting in my billet at 4.30 p.m. I was rather surprised to see Ball, coming down the road.

He gave me orders to report to Brigade at La Gorgue for a Trench Mortar course. I packed up hastily and went back in the mess cart which had brought him, taking Weeks, my servant, with me. Brigade met me very coldly, saying the battalion had as usual misread orders, and I was not wanted until to-morrow. I went back in the mess cart all the way to La Fosse and fixed myself up in Ball's billet, had dinner, and talked afterwards with Symons and Evers.

Sunday, 25th June.
Breakfast at 9.30 in B company mess, where I found I was the first arrival. Afterwards I went to an open-air Celebration, arriving just in time to avoid the skimped Mattins and address, which I had intended. After lunch I went away again in the mess cart with my servant to La Gorgue, and reported at Brigade. This time they were more cordial, and I finally got on to an L.G. omnibus painted grey with some of the advertisements still shewing, with about five other officers to St. Venant. We had a delightful drive, all the nicer as it took us practically out of sound of the guns. On arrival we reported to the First Army School of Mortars and were given billets. The owner of mine was out for the afternoon and did not return till seven ; but when I did get in I found it a very good one ; again a bed with sheets. We mess in a room in the Hotel de Ville, rather a motley collection, whose conversation is not of the cleanest.

My new Auto-strop came to-day—most acceptable, since my servant broke the old one a week or so ago, in his frenzied efforts to clean it.

Monday, 26th June.
The T.M. course began to-day. We are light mortars, i.e. Stokes' gun, a comparatively new invention. The course includes a 4" mortar and a 3.7" smoke gun, neither of which two are ever used now. We work from 9 till nearly 1, and again 2-4 ; 5 to 6 is recapitulation or some such nonsense.

At 6.0 p.m. I found a piano in a shop and played on it till 8.0, recalling bits of the Emperor and the Brahms B flat. There was a terrific downpour of rain in the evening, and I got wet through in running to my billet.

Tuesday, 27th June.
Much the same as yesterday. The water or food here doesn't seem to agree with me as much as it might. I played on the piano again in the evening.

Wednesday, 28th June—Saturday, 1st July.
Work on the course makes life fairly monotonous, and leaves little time for anything of interest except the piano in the shop. I generally go to bed early—9.30 or 10.0—as the heat is rather trying.

One day I went to what seemed to be a school presided over by nuns where they gave us a bath in a great round wooden tub. And one day we saw a barge go down the canal full of wounded. They say they take spinal and head cases down to the coast that way.

LAVENTIE

Sunday, 2nd July.

Left St. Venant at 9 o'clock : absurdly early. 11 o'clock would have done just as well and been more convenient. The bus took us to La Gorgue and there we reported to Division, who sent us on to Brigade. Here Perry-Jones, the Staff Captain, told us to go on to Laventie and report to the 183rd L.T.M.B. That settles it. I shall not go back to the regiment, and now I don't care, in fact I am rather pleased. Life was not very satisfactory there.

Then Sage, Vacher and I sweltered along the pavé road from La Gorgue to Laventie, arriving in time for tea. We found the 183rd L.T.M.B. in the person of Capt. Thacker, come from the 4th Gloucesters. This place is a pleasant little town with a row of trees down each side of the main street. The station is at one end, and four cross roads and a battered church at the other. Our billet, nearly opposite the church, includes a mess and three bedrooms between four of us. The men live further down the street. In the afternoon I walked up to the front line and back. It seems quiet enough.

Monday, 3rd July.

This seems like beginning a new life. We are a delightfully self-contained little party, and seem very independent in comparison with the infantry. At 4 p.m. Vacher and I went up the line and did a little registering on saps &c. from emplacements. We were finished by 5 o'clock. It is an extraordinary sensation to give an order and send 10 lbs. odd of explosive over some 300 yards in the hopes that it will kill somebody the other side.

The line is a better one than the Moated Grange sector, where we were last, but not so good as Neuve Chapelle. There is hardly any parades, except in the actual firebays.

For the battery officers, Thacker is young, and full of the joy of command and very reminiscent of the 4th Gloucesters and their doings in England. Sage, from the 6th Gloucesters, is rather an enigma, and doesn't say much. Vacher, 7th Wilts, 7th Worcs., is also young, even childish at times, and was at Sherborne School. He tends rather to be the life of the party being full of 'quips and cranks.' The fourth subaltern, Gascoigne, from the 7th Worcs., I can't make much out of.

Tuesday, 4th July.

Again little to do in the morning. Vacher and I went up the line at 6.0 p.m. He had two guns near bay 102 and I two near bay 64. D Coy. of the 7th Worcs. and 4th Gloucesters on the right and left respectively 'went over' at 10.30 and 1.30. The guns began at 10 and we fired slowly during the bombardment. I observed from a firebay close to my right hand gun and shouted corrections to Pte. Archer, who seemed quite to be enjoying it. Watching the performance with me was Capt. Butcher of the 7th Worcs. standing head and shoulders over the parapet, marking with rifle cartridges the direction of the flash of Bosch machine guns. I didn't care about standing up so boldly, but I didn't wish to be outdone by him and so stood up beside him. We got a good deal back in one way and another, shrapnel and 4.2's and 5.9's on the front line and behind.

The guns went on more or less continuously till 3.0 a.m. We had nothing to do for the second raid, and so I went down and joined Vacher at the H.Q. dugout near Drury Lane and there sat with him in a little crack of a trench about six feet long and two wide. He was joined by Lt. Hayes, a gunner on Medium T.M.'s, who amused us considerably. He has been out some time. The dugout itself was full of wounded, three being accommodated. Only about three were killed, I believe, but some fifteen or twenty wounded. We had no casualties. About 4.30 a.m. Vacher and I struggled out down Drury Lane and Strand, and arrived in billets rather the worse for wear.

Wednesday, 5th July.
We breakfasted at 1 p.m. and spent a very leisurely day.

Thursday, 6th July.
At 11.0 a.m. we went up into the line to do our turn of duty—that is Vacher and myself. We share a dugout by day with Hayes, the medium T.M. It is by no means a bad one, about eight feet square and contains two beds and a table. Hayes has a special kind of hammock chair constructed out of sandbags. We had no firing to do and sat a good deal talking to Hayes who is a great source of joy. At dusk we took our guns out to a dugout close to White House at the bottom of the Strand. It was used as an ammunition store and is rather damp and beastly. We talked a little with Manuel, the doctor of the 7th Worcs., who are in now. He is a pleasant, soft voiced Scot, who matriculated at Edinburgh and knows A. V. Dill. The latter, he tells me, is in the Army, engaged on bacteriological research.

Friday, 7th July.
Back to the line at 7 a.m. It rained this morning, and part of the afternoon, making the duckboards very slippery. Some slight excitement was caused by the Bosch trying to knock out a 'medium' emplacement with half a dozen salvoes of 5.9's. He did not succeed in hitting it, but made a great mess all round.

Saturday, 8th July.
Better day than yesterday. Hayes went out of the line and was relieved by King, who sleeps in the front line in pyjamas. We did a little shooting from the right hand gun in bay 64 this afternoon and got some aerial torpedoes back. They are quite small things, bursting on impact and don't do very much harm unless quite close to you. One fell ten yards from me in the open, which I hardly felt.

Sunday, 9th July.
Quiet day.

Monday, 10th July.
We did a little shooting at 2 p.m. to the interest of Capt. Odgers, who had just come into the line with the 8th Worcs. There was nothing sent back. I went down to A company and saw the 'old Gent.' and Symons. I also met Evers, who was very proud because his snipers claimed two victims this morning.

Every night our guns behind—18-pdrs and hows.—fire a "drill" from 10.0 to 10.30, and the Hun retaliates on the front line and supports. This time with more than his usual luck he dropped a 5.9 in a firebay near Rotten Row killing instantly Lt. Ball of the Devons and 8th Worcs., and his runner, Pte. Wheeler of No. 8 platoon. I am very sorry about Ball as he was a good fellow.

Tuesday, 11th July.
I hear the 8th Worcs. have a new C.O.—Col. Bilton, a Scot. Checkitts has returned to England. Who should I meet in the line this morning but O. C. Constable, late of C2 Marlborough. He has come from the special reserve and now belongs to A company. We were relieved by the other half battery at 11.0 a.m. and went back to Laventie without delay. After lunch I bathed in a brewery in a small tub.

Wednesday, 12th—Friday, 14th July.
These three days can be grouped, since, being out of the line one did nothing but read, write, eat and sleep : these four absorbing all one's energies.

Saturday, 15th July.
After an early tea I went up to the line at 5.0 p.m. and made ready for a small gas show. They have the oddest code words for these entertainments, such as "the King has been pleased to approve of your appointment," which, with a time given, meant that you were to be ready for whatever was going to happen. This particular performance began at 8.0 and we had to loose off for ten minutes or so. The wind was only just favourable, and in fact some of the stuff blew across to our own lines further north, where they curve round. Nothing happened for a few minutes : probably the Hun didn't notice it or thought it was the English playing the fool again. However, when he really smelt something he began to put over quite a good deal. Our guns were very quiet. We sat in a little bit of trench by the dugout and listened to the Huns salvoes of 4.2's—one shell just in No-Man's land, one more or less on the parapet, and two just behind. These he dotted all the way down at intervals of about thirty yards. It was more than usually interesting judging the distance of the last salvo, and wondering if the next would be just on or off the critical spot. We finished our gas by about 9.0 p.m., but the Hun went on just the same till about midnight.

Sunday, 16th July.
Vacher and I crawled out of the line about 3.0 a.m. and lurched into our beds in Laventie. We spent a very peaceful morning. Thacker informed us that an attack was impending and we must toss up for going over. Without tossing I think we arranged that Vacher and I should go over on the day, chiefly on the grounds that neither of us were married, though Vacher was engaged at the time.

In the afternoon Vacher and I went up again by Drury Lane, and had to transfer the guns from there to the left battalion sector. This involved passing Rotten Row—most appropriate name—which the Huns had strafed properly last night, pushing in two or three firebays and leaving

any who passed that way open to view. However we managed to get along and installed the guns. Then we had to go out again by Picantin down on the left to get shells up for them. The dump was at Red House, about a quarter of a mile beyond Tilleloy St., and three quarters at least in all. However the need was urgent and I decided to bring two boxes down by each man : each box holds three shells and weighs forty pounds. The men all started with their loads, grumbling of course. However only three of the party, including myself, managed to finish the journey. The others left one on the way, for which I made them go back. However I never wish to do such a thing again, and will never ask the men to. The Huns had strafed Rifleman's Avenue, the trench we came down by, pretty badly, and there were some sad sights there. I spent the night in the emplacement with Sage and was pretty cold, having only my oil sheet over me.

Monday, 17th July.
A big show was supposed to begin this morning at 4 a.m., but owing to heavy mist and the consequent difficulty for the gunners, zero was postponed till 8 a.m. I think we were all rather on edge, as this was to be a big affair. I was, certainly, and disliked having it put off. Again it was postponed till eleven o'clock, and then indefinitely. Some people did not get their orders in time and I stopped two medium T.M.'s who had begun pooping off at 11 o'clock under the impression the show was begun.

However this final postponement meant that we had to go for more ammunition, which meant going up and down the communication trenches several times again. Any ordinary ones may not be so bad ; in fact those behind Neuve Chapelle are much nicer. These, however, being straight in front of the Aubers Ridge, are raked by the enemy all the way. He can see the smallest beetle on the duckboards, let alone men struggling with ammunition. To add to all this our own 18-pounders were pooping off all the time and the Hun retaliates on the communication trenches. A further point, they are made so insanely. They dig down about five feet, just not enough to cover the average man, and then lay duckboards down on posts raised some eighteen inches to two feet above the level of the trench. The result is you walk along what someone described as a 'kind of elevated railway,' with everything above your waist belt visible to enemy snipers, who are not slow to appreciate this. I heard someone say of Sutherland Avenue, which he was walking up for the first time that he was appalled to find himself raised several feet above natural ground level, and gazing not only at the Hun trenches but even at our own wire at the bottom of our own parapet. To give us a bit of a rest, Vacher and I, who were to ' go over,' went out of the line at 7 p.m. and back to Laventie.

Tuesday, 18th July.
Got up late and had a very easy and comfortable morning and afternoon. We went back to the line at 5.0 p.m. and spent a fairly quiet night in the emplacement.

Wednesday, 19th July.
Nice warm day. I noticed this much quite early, but could not say

at all what it was like later on. Zero was at 11.0 a.m. I had no firing to do, as I was to go over, and kept my men close up in the firebays with the guns handy. I was to go with the 4th Gloucesters, and spent the time on the left of Rifleman's Avenue. The men were very crowded, eight or even twelve in a firebay. The guns began at 11.0 and went on till 6 p.m. I didn't notice them very much, though I was dully aware of a terrific noise. I seem unable to remember distinctly how I passed those seven hours. Part of the time was spent sitting on a mud-scraper outside an infantry company headquarters near the top of Sutherland Avenue. I don't remember seeing Vacher at all. We got a lot back, mostly shrapnel on the front line, but not nearly so much as we sent over. We had, I was told afterwards, twenty 12-inch guns behind us, some naval 9.2's, heavy trench mortars, and all kinds of other things. The Hun shrapnel reaped a pretty rich harvest with the men so close together in the firebays. Then 6 o'clock came, still broad daylight, and the attack was due to start. We were to go out by the sally ports—more or less screened holes in the parapet. Well, the Hun had m.g.'s set on all these. The attack was to be in four waves or lines : we were to go in the fourth. Casualties had been such that they were forced to reorganise the waves just before starting and things were a bit confused. The Hun had put down a good barrage of shrapnel and H.E. on No Man's land and fired his m.g.'s continuously. The first two waves went out, and those who did not stay in a heap just outside the sally-port crawled on down a ditch running across to the Hun line. Some of the third wave went, much depleted, and then came our turn. I was wearing a kind of jacket for carrying four shells. This I took off, not caring for the risk of having a fuse cut by a bullet, and just then the attack was stopped. One or two had got as far as the Hun wire, none had got any further, and most could never come back. Altogether it must be owned that the attack was a dead failure. We heard afterwards that the Australians on our left got over and stayed in the Hun lines all night.

Those of the 4th Gloucesters who were left were in a pretty shaky condition, and I had to take my men up into a firebay to do sentry for the night. None of us were too cheery, in fact my nerves were in a beastly state, I'm afraid. We had only had one casualty that I knew of. I put one man up against the parapet to look over as sentry, and another by his side for company. The rest of us huddled down in a very narrow bit of fire trench close by. Sentries were changed every half hour. One man's nerve was quite gone, and he could only sit, shaking uncontrollably all the time. Two others were nearly the same, but we employed ourselves in discussing our respective peace-time jobs. I now know quite a lot about weaving carpets in Kidderminster. All these little schemes were going quite well until the Hun began sending whizz-bangs over just where we were. It didn't matter so much when they cleared the parapet and burst some ten yards behind. That was infinitely remote by then. But what was disconcerting was his decreased elevation, which made him knock the top sandbag off our parapet. Finally one burst within about six feet of Bowater, who was acting sentry, and threw him down into the trench among us. His companion did a rapid exit down a short entry trench

on to the duckboards beyond and had to be fetched back. Bowater was rather shaken up, so I took a turn at sentry, with one of the men sitting close by. I discovered two of the Gloucesters in a corner of the trench, one of whom turned out to be a Devonshire man. He said he came from some place I knew quite well, but which I forget now, and I was just getting into an interesting conversation with him when word came along for the Gloucesters to go out. He broke off in the middle of a sentence, and with an Oh ! dashed round the corner out of the trench with no further ceremony.

Thursday, 20th July.
By 2 a.m. the 7th Worcesters had relieved the Gloucesters, so we came down out of the firebay and I sent the men to their dugouts, except the man with nerves whom I sent out, with Bowater as escort. I lay down in the gun emplacement.

The day was comparatively quiet. Vacher went out and Sage came in to relieve him. The guns still kept up a fairly constant bombardment, but I did no firing. I think the Bosche front line was evacuated. During the night a good many wounded were brought in from No Man's land—people they had been unable to get in by day.

Friday, 21st July.
The day was again quiet, and the guns actually stopped firing for a few hours. I went to sleep in the afternoon, and was treated to a good old-fashioned nightmare. At 6.30 p.m. we were relieved by the other half battery and very thankfully came out to Laventie, going, by popular vote, by Picantin, as the least strafed communication trench. I sent my servant out and he bought three bottles of Veuve Cliquot, which we drank. Symons and Constable came in later and helped to finish it. Then I went to bed.

Saturday, 22nd July.
After our strenuous time we did not feel inclined to exert ourselves too much. Sage and I rode over on push bikes to La Gorgue and had a very nice hot bath in a factory. French women work in part of it, spinning something like flax, which I believe they make into sandbags. After the bath we went on to Estaires for tea in the Hotel de Commerce, quite a good place. I dined in Laventie with A company of the 8th Worcesters ; Symons and Constable being there. They walked back with me about nine o'clock and we had the interesting spectacle of four horses from an artillery caisson galloping wildly down the street in pairs, having run away. They were stopped some way down the road by our billet.

Sunday, 23rd July.
Read all the morning and afternoon. After dinner I went a walk with Thacker, our O.C., into La Gorgue and Estaires. On the way we were struck all of a heap by being offered a lift by Hereward Wake, G.S.O. 1 of the Division. Unfortunately we were too astonished to accept. However we had a good walk.

Monday, 24th July.

I went up to the line with a message, taking Weeks with me. This was my only activity.

Tuesday, 25th July.

Had my hair cut in the afternoon at a little shop here. I went up the line at 5.0 p.m. to take over on the left of Rotten Row. I have four guns and am alone on my sector. The dugout is a very uncomfortable one : you can only just sit up, and have to crawl in on hands and knees.

We'nesday, 26th July.

Nothing much to do. I met a man in the line, Capt. Wyatt, who was at Marlborough in my time, now in command of a company of the 4th Gloucesters. He belongs properly to the Northamptons. He was out here before in the battle of Neuve Chapelle. I asked him about Col. Fisher Rowe, and oddly enough he had been hit at the same time and followed Lawrence's stretcher to the dressing station. Another man I met, also in the 4th Gloucesters, was G. D. A. Fox of Keble, the pianist. He has just come up into the line for the first time. It is great rot bringing a man like that up.

I did some shooting at 12.0 and 1.0 a.m. and had some shrapnel back, but not much.

Thursday, 27th July.

From 8.0 to 8.30 this morning was a combined artillery and T.M. shoot on the Wick salient, an unfortunate piece of German line opposite Rotten Row. This became rather famous afterwards as " the Breakfast Shoot." Our heavy T.M. came into action, and I've never seen such explosions. It shook the ground where we were, four hundred yards away, and sent up duckboards and bits of concrete dugouts in a great fountain I should think a hundred feet high. The Huns put a lot of 5.9's on to Tilleloy, looking for the heavy, I suppose. I could see the shell drop from about 100 feet up, and then the cloud of earth, &c., a second or two before I heard the explosion. A good many of his shells were duds.

We spent the afternoon getting up ammunition. Then about tea time we put a 6-inch howitser on to the Sugar Loaf, another salient. No firing at night, and I slept long.

Friday, 28th July.

This morning the 8th Worcesters sent over some rifle grenades about 8.0 a.m., which provoked the Hun to plaster Rotten Row for about half an hour with 5.9's and shrapnel. Later they sent some stuff over to Laventie without doing much damage. I saw Wyatt again and went through Rotten Row to see Sage. They have churned it up properly.

Saturday, 29th July.

Very hot to-day. Nothing much to do. Gascoigne relieved me and my gun teams at 6.30 p.m. We went out by Picantin.

Sunday and Monday, 30th and 31st July, Tuesday, 1st August.

Very hot again. Sage and I rode over to La Gorgue in the afternoon

and had a bath, and then 'tea' at the Hotel de Commerce, Estaires, where we had little biscuits and coffee.

Monday was again hot; and Tuesday. That afternoon Sage and I went a walk and sat in the shade of a hedge wishing the war were over.

Wednesday, 2nd August.

Blazing hot day. I went up to the right sector at 5 p.m. relieving Vacher. We had a shoot on from 12.0 to 1.0 a.m. The Hun strafed Tilleloy with 4.2's and stopped as soon as we did.

Thursday, 3rd August.

Quiet hot day. On these days one either sits in the dugout or wanders slowly up the line visiting company commanders and any friends who happen to be about.

Friday, 4th August.

Slept last night from 12.0 to 8.0 a.m.; not so bad for the front line. While in the line this morning I met Symons and Evers. Presently Bomford joined us and we all four borrowed rifles and solemnly fired one round apiece over the parapet (not staying up long enough to take much aim) in honour of the anniversary of the beginning of the war. The gunners woke up a bit at lunch time and created a slight disturbance. Great preparations for a small gas show which was fortunately cancelled towards evening. The code word this time was "Jorrocks." King, the medium T.M., came up for it and slept in the line. Hayes, his predecessor, was hit slightly on the 19th.

Saturday, 5th August.

A nice easy day with nothing to do beyond carrying some shells and removing empty boxes. The Edinburgh Review came to-day and proved quite interesting. I had asked for it to be sent out. After dark I took L.-Cpl. Archer with me and went reconnoitring in No Man's land for a gun position to be used a few days hence. We found a good site in a heavy T.M. hole just beyond our own wire—one which had dropped short on the 19th, and I drew an elaborate map for Thacker to shew how to get there.

Sunday, 6th August.

Vacher relieved me at 7 p.m. and we got out by Masselot Street without mishap. We had not been out five minutes before the news came in that Gascoigne had wounded himself with his revolver. That meant that I should have to take his place to-morrow—just my luck. To add to the annoyance the Bosch started to shell Laventie, putting down shrapnel on to the cross roads. Sage and I were so annoyed that we left our supper and went a walk out behind the railway. They stopped by the time we came back, and we finished our food in peace. It is too much of a good thing to be shelled in billets when just come out of the line.

Monday, 7th August.

Thacker and I up to the line at 5 p.m. I went out with a gun at 10 p.m., taking a corporal, two men, and four infantry as a covering party for a raid by the 8th Worcesters. We struggled along through the wire,

I carrying the baseplate. Once I dropped down with my face on a 'gooseberry' at a Hun very light, and tore holes in my hands. We arrived at last and mounted the gun. The raid did not succeed as the Hun opened m.g.'s on them before they were fairly started, so we scrambled back soon after midnight. Thacker and I arrived in billets by 3.30 a.m., and I slept as I was in my clothes.

Perhaps a list of my two gun teams will not be without interest. They were :—

L.-Cpl.	Hunt	L.-Cpl.	Archer
Pte.	Bowater	Pte.	Hackett
	Skerratt		Beach
	Britton		Massey
	White		Hughes

Tuesday, 8th August.
After lunch I went to an ironmonger's where there is a piano, picking up Symons on the way, and played bits of the Brahms B flat Concerto, which he knew from Maldon and Brentwood days. The score has just come, sent out with Brahms' C minor symphony and Cesar Franck's symphony. I went back with Symons to tea.

Wednesday, 9th August.
The brigade was relieved to-day. I went back, ride and tie with Durkin, an understudy to Brigade-Signals, to La Gorgue, where we are billeted on the edge of the town, close to a level crossing. I share a bedroom with Sage. There is no furniture save the two beds and one chair, and the owners have to pass through our bedroom to get to theirs. Fortunately they both go to bed and get up very early, so it does not so much matter. Sage, Durkin and I had baths and then tea in Estaires. We looked in vain for a piano. A great interest is the train. One came by, complete with engine, in the evening, and we all stood in the road to watch, and called the servants. A further addition to the mess is Clarke from the 6th Gloucesters, attached to the Brigade as "tramways." He is an amusing fellow, and was A.D.C. to Gen. Drummond, "Southern Command."

Thursday, 10th August.
We had a little rain to-day. It is my day for duty, involving one parade of gun drill in the morning, most of which I have forgotten since the St. Venant course, and another short one after lunch. That was all, and a good thing too.

Friday, 11th August.
Gun drill in the morning. After lunch I rode to Merville to look for Col. Lawrence Rowe's grave, but could not find it. I saw Tiddy's name in the casualty list, killed by a shell in the line yesterday.

Saturday, 12th August.
Gun drill as usual.

Sunday, 13th August.
I took the battery to church in the morning. Besides ourselves were

the Brigade signallers, some R.A.M.C., and the 8th Worcesters—quite a crowd. Fenn took the service, the 8th padre, and preached about Timothy, rather well. I think it is the first compulsory church parade I have been to out here.

Monday, 14th August.
Went out early towards Merville and did an attack with the 7th Worcesters in some fields outside the town. The M.G.'s were there too, very bored, like ourselves. Major-Gen. Mackenzie turned up in the middle and seemed interested.

The heat or the smells have made me rather odd inside, so I have to be careful.

Tuesday, 15th August.
Lunched very gently with Vacher and Tanner, from Brigade in Estaires. We found a piano and played on it. The Hotel de Ville is a good place, and you can get a very good lunch. The centre table is always taken up by some curious old Frenchmen, one of whom wears the red ribbon of the Legion d'Honneur. We had a good deal of rain to-day.

Wednesday, 16th August.
After a fairly early breakfast Vacher and I went on a bus to Steenbecque, with a lot of others, to see the XIth Corps Sniping School. It was a very pleasant drive through the outskirts of St. Venant and along by the canal. On the way there we passed the artillery of some Scotch division, going up to Armentières, people said. The road was very congested, and so, at a turning, our driver asked how much mo e of them there was. " Oh, about five miles, I think," was the answer, and so we turned off and went by another road through the Forêt de Nieppe, which is quite pretty. We turned off the main road just short of Aire and arrived at the school about 11.0 a.m. It was not very interesting and hardly concerned us, and I failed to get very enthusiastic over it.

On returning to the estaminet where we had left the bus we found it gone, and were told the driver had gone into Aire for lunch. Someone went to fetch him, and meanwhile four of us had a competition throwing little feathered darts at a target on the wall, over which I lost a couple of francs. Then the bus came, and we started home, getting in at 3.0 p.m. We spend the evenings eating large purple plums and listening to Clarke tell stories of life on the Manchester Guardian of which he was a sub-editor, I think.

Thursday, 17th August.
Another wet day. Vacher and I lunched in Estaires and were joined by the Old Gent who was, as usual, very talkative. After lunch we did a little shopping.

Friday, 18th August.
A perfect summer day. We moved to Les Huit Maisons, further south and not far from Croix Barbée. Clarke, Vacher and I walked over together, Sage going up into the line. We are in a farm—a very small one—with a very picturesque little courtyard and dungheap in the middle.

It is really a very sweet little place. The mess-room, which is also a bedroom for me and Durkin, the signals officer, is about ten feet square. There is just room for two beds, two chairs, and a table. I like it, as it is cosy and clean, but the others say it is too small. After lunch Clarke and I played one of his war games on a big map of Northern France, using matches to represent divisions. Operations culminated in a big battle near Lille, where he beat me handsomely.

Saturday, 19th August.
I went up to the line in the morning to take a message to Sage, in the Neuve Chapelle sector. Our headquarters are not in the line this time, but in some old dugouts near rail-head, at the bottom of Hun Street. In the afternoon I tried to sketch the courtyard of the billet.

Sunday, 20th August.
I left the billet at 10 a.m. and took over from Sage at 12, going up the " covered way " alongside the La Bassée road, ' covered,' as someone said, only by the Hun machine guns at night.

The line in front here is in rather a bad state. The Hun came over not so long ago and left his mark very unmistakably. When he does raid he does it in style.

We had a quiet afternoon, but at 10.30 p.m. we did a bit of a show, firing some six hundred shells. Thacker came up for it, and slept with me in the dugout.

Monday, 21st August.
A chilly morning. I went up to the line once or twice to look round. Up at the right hand end by the top of Hazard street is a fine dud heavy Minnie. The casing is of aluminium, about 11 inches in diameter and two feet high, tapering slightly at the top, with a nose cap : an interesting sight. They have put up a notice board—" do not touch." It will be rather a ticklish job unscrewing the fusehead. One meets with a good deal of unintentional humour in the notices up the line, such as " It is DANGEROUS to pass here," or " DANGER, do not loiter," &c., &c. I went right down Orchard trench and along the Rue du Bois with Cpl. Hunt. We had to go along the ditch most of the way, as we were otherwise in full view of the Hun. We came across an English 6-inch Naval shell dud, about five feet long. In the afternoon I went up with a map and glasses to Port Arthur, near the La Bassée road, where you get a splendid view down south. I could make out Cambrin and Fosse 8, and I think Loos with its towers. La Bassée was quite plain : I could see the smoke of a German train in the distance : altogether a most interesting view.

Tuesday, 22nd August.
Good night. I went up round the line in the morning. Vacher relieved me at 12, and I arrived back in time for lunch. There was an aeroplane duel close up above the billet in the afternoon, both planes firing their machine guns like mad. The Hun escaped that time, but later on one was brought down by the A.A. guns.

We are close to an observation balloon here, and it is quite interesting

through glasses. They seem to sway about a lot in the wind, and one hears that the people in them are often seasick at first.

Wednesday, 23rd August.
Rode over to La Gorgue in the morning with Thacker for a bath, and got very hot : he will ride so fast. We came back for lunch, and I spent the afternoon reading ' Blinds down,' a not very interesting book by Vachell.

Thursday, 24th August.
Read again. Clarke and I played two war games on the map in the afternoon, both of which he won. I'm not much good at that kind of thing and he is, but it is quite interesting.

Friday, 25th August.
Went to the Holy Communion, which the Brigade Padre celebrated in the orchard close by. A good many of the battery attended. Later Clarke and I played another war game, and I finished ' Blinds down ' : an unsatisfactory book.

Saturday, 26th August.
I relieved Sage this morning and then carried the guns along the front line to the left, as our sector now stretches from the village of Neuve Chapelle to Winchester street, involving a carry of one of the guns of about two miles : no joke along the duckboards. Headquarters is now at Hush Hall, behind the Chateau. Hush Hall, Baluchi Road, Neuve Chapelle, is quite a fine address. It is a very good elephant dugout, tucked in behind the ruins of a farm, and was once a battalion headquarters. I share it rather as a paying guest with the machine gunners, the real owners. At present E. G. Wardrop is up, a very large easy going fellow. I forgot to bring my coat up and consequently was very cold in the night. The rats are rather alarming. They rampage all over the dugout and seem to be trying to carry our beds round the table in the middle.

Sunday, 27th August.
I washed very comfortably and shaved at about 10 a.m. and then went round the guns. On the way to the left guns I passed the new Mauquissart crater which the Huns put up a few weeks ago under a company of the Warwicks. It is larger than the Duck's Bill and makes quite a little hill on the skyline. They have made firebays, and a circulating trench round the near lip of the crater, which has some thirty feet of water in it.

In the afternoon we had a combined shoot with the mediums. I started at bay 200, just on the right of Chateau road and made my way along the duckboards. They dropped a Minnie about ten yards behind me as I passed Chateau road, so I hastened my steps, moving perhaps with less dignity than speed. Beyond Sign Post lane I ran into a barrage of aerial torpedoes which were rather disturbing—in fact, to be blunt, " I had the wind up " rather badly. However I wrote my Tactical Progress Report in a firebay, and when things got a bit quieter went back to Bigwood's company headquarters on the left of Chateau road, where he offered me tea. I was just going to begin when a Minnie dropped just

short of the dugout and shook it as a dog does a rat. There were four or five people in the dugout, and most of them found important business elsewhere at once. I wanted my tea rather badly and so sat on, with my battle bowler on, as Vacher calls it, until, half a minute later, the dugout was half filled with bits of mud and muck from another which had just dropped ' over ' this time. I left my tea then and slipped down Chateau road as quick as I could, getting past the awkward point just in time to hear another come and drop in the mud in much the same place. My coat had come up by this time so I had a good night.

Monday, 28th August.
I got up in a fairly leisurely way and was relieved by Vacher at 11 a.m., coming out by 1 p.m. in time for lunch ; our headquarters being now at Laventie, not in the old place but near Cockshy house on the Rue du Paradis. Clarke is still with us. I sleep with Sage over the road in a most pestilential, flyridden, cupboard of a place.

Tuesday, 29th August.
A wet day. I went to the ironmonger's shop in the morning with Sage and played nearly all the Brahms B flat concerto to him for his sins, finishing by improvising a little, hymns, &c., which he seemed to like.

In the afternoon I rode into La Gorgue with Thacker, where we bathed, and got some money, and had tea in Estaires. We rode home in pouring rain, which continued all the evening, and all next day.

Thursday, 31st August.
In the afternoon I went to the ironmonger's and played. They produced some Chopin for me, waltzes, scherzos, polonaises, all much too hard, which I tried. Capt. A. E. Ball, on Brigade, and Bernheim, the interpreter, both good people, came in. The latter was rather amusing talking the slang French, ' no bon,' ' napooh,' &c.

Friday, 1st September.
Up to the line in the morning to Hush Hall again. The Hun shelled a cottage near by with 25 5.9's at tea time, during which we retired to B lines and looked on. Just now we are on bully beef and biscuits, so before coming up I sent Weeks to buy some bread. He announced that the infantry had collared it all. I stopped at an estaminet on the way up and, asking, was told it would be ' cuit en dix minutes.' I asked if some could not be had a little sooner than the rest, but the woman shook her head and told me that ' tout le monde ' was waiting for it—some two old men and a boy, sitting round the room. We could not wait and had to go on, breadless. After our tea, which we finished at 6.0, cold, we went to see the damage to the cottage, which did not amount to much, and no one lives there. Dinner at 8.0 of machonochie, pears and pineapple, and tea.

Saturday, 2nd September.
A glorious morning. At 5 a.m., before it was quite light, Wardrop and I went again to see yesterday's 5.9 holes : some were quite big. Then we went across into Neuve Chapelle and had a look at his brickfields

emplacement. We wandered on from there round by the church and back down the lane to Mogg's Hole. It is all very beautiful and peaceful at that time in the morning, no one firing at all, and a slight mist over everything.

The day was quiet and we did not do very much. At 6.0 p.m. the Hun put a couple of 4.2's on to the house at the back, and so we moved off at once down Baluchi to B lines. We were just clear in time to avoid three salvoes, sent over as quick as lightning. The dugout was not touched.

Sunday, 3rd September.

I came out in the morning and met Gen. Mackenzie in Baluchi road on my way. Such are the interests of our lives here.

Monday, 4th September.

Had to get up early to-day, as I am on a physical drill course which begins at 9.15 on the further edge of La Gorgue. I find it is being run by a Sgt. Child of the 8th Worcesters, whom I know quite well. There is a queer collection of people on the course : a good number of gunners and their N.C.O.'s, two aged R.A.M.C. captains, one other T.M.B. from 184th Brigade, and a pleasant machine gunner, Cox-Walker by name, from 182nd. I had lunch at the Hotel de Ville, Estaires, for 3 f. 50, and then went back for the afternoon performance which finished at 4 p.m. We are alternately drilled by the instructor and drill each other. The latter is sometimes amusing, especially as a strict adherence to the precise form of words is insisted on ; otherwise the spell is broken. I rode back along the La Bassée road.

Tuesday, 5th September.

Rain all day : roads very muddy. We did our work in the divisional theatre, which was very cold and draughty. I caught something of a chill.

Wednesday, 6th September.

Feeling rather cheap and peevish to-day. I had a bath in the luncheon interval, and then got leave off from Child and returned. I found a new member of the mess in Lt. H. H. Field, replacing Sage, who fell off his bicycle when I was last up the line and was removed to hospital. Field is young, somewhat boisterous, and comes from Manchester via Shrewsbury School. I retired to bed early.

Thursday, 7th September.

To the course again. We had a sort of an exam. after lunch and had to drill each other. I came back then and had tea, afterwards going to the piano at the ironmonger's, where I enjoyed myself.

Friday, 8th September.

I sat in most of the day and tried to write some counterpoint exercises as variations on a five finger tune. There was a raid on in the evening to which we listened from the garden. My name has gone in for a transfer to the M.G.C., and I hope to get it. It seems a more desirable life than my present one.

Saturday, 9th September.

Beautiful day. I went up into the line in the morning to take over from Field. The sector has again shifted slightly to the left, and headquarters is now off Winchester trench, quite a nice little whitewashed dugout, in an old support line. I visited Smith of the machine gunners in the afternoon in Winchester post and had tea there. Between 9 and 10 p.m. we let off about an hundred shells without getting much back. The Tactical Progress Report, timed 11 p.m., I give as a specimen.

To Capt. Thacker.
From 2/Lt. H. M. Adams.

I saw the Infantry Company Commanders and they said they wanted to send out patrols and do wiring, &c., and besought me to fire for a limited time only. So I went on your first orders and fired from 9-10.

L-Cpl. Chudleigh, firing from bay 75—the gun nearest Winchester on the left—fired 50 shells at and round M. 24 d. 4.0, range 400. There was no retaliation. The infantry fired a few rifle grenades into the crater in front of B company as the Huns were said to be in it, and had a few shells back.

L-Cpl. Mitchelmore fired from bay 15, by the Duck's Bill, 50 shells, at M. 36 a. 3.2, range 360. The Hun retaliated towards the end with a few rifle grenades, but these may have been meant for the infantry who were also firing them.

Re ammunition. The Hun has smashed up the railway, and so nothing can go by it at present. Most of the trucks are on the front line side of the smash!

11.0 p.m., 9.ix.1916.

Sunday, 10th September.

Very quiet. Nothing to do all day. Took a gun down to the Duck's Bill and fired a few rounds at 2 a.m. 11th, when we sent up a small mine, but there was no reply. It hardly seems as if the Hun were holding his front line just here, though there are always plenty of them when anyone goes over to see.

Monday, 11th September.

Quiet morning. We were relieved, by the help of a good deal of bad language, by 3 p.m.; and then started off for Merville on brigade rest. The men pushed the guns on handcarts and I went independently on a bicycle. I stopped on the way at an 18-pounder battery near the La Bassée road and was given tea. Then, near La Gorgue I came up with Major Bartleet, late of D company 8th Worcesters, now second in command of the 6th Gloucesters. I walked with him into the town, and then rode off along the canal towpath to Merville. I am billeted with Vacher, in quite a respectable bedroom. We mess in a house near by. Clarke is no longer with us as he has to be near brigade who stay in La Gorgue.

I have never been in Merville before but once. It is quite a good town, untouched by the war, as far as one can see, and possessing a handsome church, two teashops, a 'Burberry's' place, E.F.C. canteen, two hospitals,

two watchmakers, &c., &c. A parcel of food came from home this evening, containing chicken and ham, but the chicken unfortunately had been too long on the road.

Tuesday, 12th September.
I got up very late this morning after my exertions of yesterday, and Vacher and I went to have breakfast in a patisserie in the town, of coffee and cakes, at about 12 o'clock. At 3 p.m. he and I rode into La Gorgue for some money from the Field Cashier, and a bath. We also went to see a relief model of the Fauquissart sector in the Div. H.Q. garden. This was quite interesting. Anderson, the corps commander, came in while we were there, with a train of satellites and so we came away. Pritchard, C. H., of the 4th Gloucesters, came to dine. He has just come out with a draft. I had met him before once or twice, at Brentwood and Epping.

Wednesday, 13th September.
A rather wet day. I went into the town in the morning, doing a little shopping, and left my watch to be mended. I met G. A. K. Hervey, now R.T.O. here, who was in B2 at Marlborough with me, and was given an invitation to dinner. After lunch I read Mrs. de la Pasture's 'The Grey Knight,' which I bought in the town; and after tea played the piano in the pub. by the station.

Thursday, 14th September.
In the morning I had to take a few men down to La Gorgue for a gas demonstration. We put on our helmets and went into a hut where they turned on the gas: then, in a weak moment I stupidly told the man we were L.T.M.B.'s and had the box respirators as well, which the infantry did not; so we had to go through the performance again. However we got back in time for lunch.

I dined with Hervey. He was out when I arrived, so I read a new collection of 'Poems of To-day,' which is rather good. Hervey arrived in due course and we had a very pleasant dinner. He has some very interesting things to tell. He started life as an officer's servant in the Artists' Rifles, and had the most delightful time, he said. He has never yet been in a front line trench. He was R.T.O. at Bethune and then moved up here a week or two ago—soon after they began to shell the other place. A wonderful life.

Friday, 15th September.
In the morning I took 4 guns down to do " the attack " with the 7th Worcesters in a field near by where we did it before. The contrast between this and the real thing as one saw it on July 19th is so absurd, and shows how hopeless it is, beyond a certain point, in trying to rehearse such a thing. In the afternoon I went into the town and saw the 8th Worcesters rehearsing a ceremonial parade for to-morrow, when the Corps Commander comes to present ribbons to various people. I went into the church, quite a fine one, and asked about the organ. The organist is blind and likes people to come and play new tunes to him, as he remembers them, and passes them on to his congregation, I suppose. He must have a wonderful memory. Dr. Shinn, in his 'Musical Memory,'

tells a story of Mendelssohn doing something of the kind with a Liszt improvisation, but I never heard of another case. G. D. A. Fox, the organ scholar of Keble, played here the other day.

Saturday, 16th September.

At an hour's notice we packed up and went into the line. A motor lorry came and took me and four guns to La Gorgue, on the way to Neuve Chapelle, and beyond La Gorgue the driver would not go without a permit from the A.P.M. I went to the A.P.M. and he told me to go to Division. I crossed the road and asked to see the Staff Captain. Then ensued this conversation. ' Good morning, sir. I have a lorry outside and want to go in it down the La Bassée road. May I have a permit ? ' ' You've no business to have a lorry at all. Where do you come from ? ' ' 183rd Brigade sent the lorry.' ' Well they had no business to.' Here someone else produced a memo. entitling 183rd Brigade to send 183rd L.T.M.B. a motor lorry. ' Oh ! all right : well, you can't go down the La Bassée road anyhow.' I explained that Stokes' guns were heavy things and one could not carry them more than three or four miles without considerable personal inconvenience ; so finally he said I must see Marinden, A.A. and Q.M.G. Marinden is known as the pocket Napoleon, being remarkably efficient, and possessing an uncanny knowledge of other people's affairs. I saw him and repeated my tale, asking to go down as far as Rouge Croix. Even that is a good two miles behind the line. However it was no good, and I was allowed to go no further than Pont du Hem, a mile further back. Then I got my first friend to write all this down on paper and sign it ; took it across to the A.P.M., who countersigned it ; and finally presented it to the driver of the lorry, and so we went on our way. From Pont du Hem the men had to carry the guns. We arrived, after an interminable and tortoiselike journey, at the front end of Baluchi road and deposited the guns in the front line. My own headquarters are in Hush Hall again, with the machine gunners. I found Lt. A. H. Press installed, and he was joined later in the evening by F. B. Thomlinson, come from Merville, where Anderson had presented him with a Military Cross ribbon for doing clever things on July 19th.

Sunday, 17th September.

The N.C.O.'s up with me are :—

Bay 168	L.-Cpl.	Archer
200	,,	Hingley
232	Cpl.	Medland
233	L.-Cpl.	Guest.

Had a long sleep last night. We had another quiet day spent in ammunition carrying. It is very nice being a little way back from the line. There are excellent opportunities for washing here, which you don't get everywhere.

Monday, 18th September.

Did a shoot in the morning. L-Cpl. Archer had a mishap. One of his cartridges misfired and threw the shell out of the gun, but not clear of the emplacement. The fuse was lighted and so the men had only just time

to clear out before the shell exploded. The emplacement was wrecked and the gun blown up into the roof and badly damaged, otherwise no harm done.

Heavy rain all day. Everything soaked through, including myself.

Tuesday, 19th September.

Thacker came up in the morning. I went over beyond Hun street looking for some old emplacements, and found them all smashed in by shells or minnies. It is rather a bad place beyond the La Bassée road. Shoot on in the evening. No firing at night, but a lot more rain.

Wednesday, 20th September.

The rats had a regular gala night last night, squealing and fighting all over the dugout, even climbing on to my bed. We kept a candle alight but that did not seem to keep them quiet. Between 2 and 3 a.m. I went a walk round some neighbouring trenches for a little peace. Vacher relieved me soon after 10 a.m. We are now sharing mess and billets with the 183rd machine gunners, the same company that lives in Hush Hall. I am in a canvas hut with quite a good bed. I went on a bike to La Gorgue for a bath, and to Estaires for tea ; going on to Laventie to buy a special kind of purple notepaper which I had had there before, and then back in the dusk down the La Bassée road.

Thursday, 21st September.

I went out a short way in the morning looking for the " medium's " billet, which I could not find. I paid the men after lunch and then began upon a piano quintet in B flat, in an old signals notebook.

Friday, 22nd September.

Nice bright day. Very cold last night in bed. Nothing much to do. I added to the furniture in my hut by a shelf and a box and a second bed. Worked again at the quintet.

Saturday, 23rd September.

Spent the morning writing. After lunch with Thacker to Estaires, and we had a bath each. Incidentally we heard at Brigade that the expected leave is cancelled : no leave till we've been out six months. I also bought a fine new stick for 9·francs, a bamboo.

Sunday, 24th September.

In the afternoon we had a service for T.M.'s and M.G.'s by the 8th Worcester's padre, in which we were made to sing three of the most amazing hymns I have ever been fated to hear, the first being 'Crown Him with many crowns.' I hear the infantry have turned us out of Hush Hall, taking it for a company headquarters, so we shall have to look for another country seat. We shall probably move further from the line, into B lines : that is the general tendency, where possible !

Monday, 25th September.

Nice warm day. Worked at the quintet all day except for a time after tea, when I went a walk through Richebourg St. Vaast. It is in a dreadful state : more grisly than most of the places I have seen. All

the houses are smashed in, and the churchyard ploughed up like a field, with many of the graves opened up.

Tuesday, 26th September.
To La Gorgue before lunch, and had my hair cut. Tried over the quintet first movement. In the afternoon I sat in reading 'Lord Loveland discovers America.'

Wednesday, 27th September.
Lazy day.

Thursday, 28th September.
Into La Gorgue with Thacker for bath and tea.

Friday, 29th September.
Nothing to do. Read during the morning, finishing the Williamson book. Went a walk in the evening.

Saturday, 30th September.
I relieved Field in the line. Our headquarters are now in B lines. The mess is a roofed-in traverse, and the bedroom can only be entered on hands and knees sideways. Brigade have ordered now a scaled system of retaliation fire, so many for a heavy, so many for an aerial torpedo, &c., which in practice hardly comes off. The 7th Worcesters let off a bangalore torpedo under the Hun wire opposite Hun street, and I fired in support of them a few rounds, but the baseplate sank so in the soft ground that I had to stop. The Hun put a lot of heavies on to the Neb. After being out of the line for so long I find my nerves rather out of order. I finished by 2.30 a.m.

Sunday, 1st October.
Summer time ended last night. I was woken up at 5.30 a.m. for 6.30 by a fellow who had forgotten to alter his watch. Then I had to go down to Euston Post and conduct some R.E.'s up the 'covered way' to the top of Hun street, where they are going to build an emplacement. Mitchelmore, Walters and Eves fired in the early part of the night from bay 233, Chateau road and Church road. Walters and his team had just left their Chateau road emplacement when a minnie came down behind it, completely blocking it up. In fact the last fifty yards or so of Chateau road no longer exists.

Monday and Tuesday, 2nd and 3rd October.
Rained all the time. Fired a good deal both days. I am getting rather tired of the war now.

Wednesday, 4th October.
I was relieved by Vacher. A charming sunny day, of course. It never does rain when I am able to go indoors out of the way of it. I went in to La Gorgue after lunch for a bath. I also played on the piano at Brigade headquarters, now unoccupied, since there are three brigades in the line. It is quite a good baby grand Pleyel: a great treat to get such a piano undisturbed.

1916

Thursday, 5th October—Monday, 9th October.
Read and wrote. Went in to La Gorgue once or twice to the piano. Vacher came once, and once Tommy Coates looked in, Gen. Mackenzie's A.D.C., and quite a nice fellow.

Tuesday, 10th October.
Lovely day. In the afternoon the whole battery went up to the line for a raid by the 7th Worcesters. I was right away on the left, by Chateau road : for me it was a case of standing by, only. There was a brilliant moon and Hun machine guns put a very effectual stopper on the raid. I heard afterwards that Booker was killed, for which I am sorry, as he was a very good fellow : not so stupid as most. He was killed bringing in wounded, of which there were a good many. We got back by 3.30 a.m.

Wednesday, 11th October.
I stayed in bed late. Thacker came in and announced in an awestruck voice that we were booked for the Somme. I can't see that it matters much. This is getting pretty unpleasant. In the afternoon I rode off on a push bike through the mud to La Gorgue and played the piano. Then to Estaires for tea. After that I went to the cemetery and found Lawrence Rowe's grave, F. 9. I rode back against a head wind to Merville along the canal towpath and bought some Tommy cooker refills at the E.F.C. By this time it was dark, so I had to pick my way as best I could, not being able to see the sign posts, through Paradis and Fosse, getting in about 8 p.m.

Thursday, 12th October.
Went round to brigade at 10 a.m. for a gas lecture on the new " Small Box Respirator." Spent the afternoon writing letters, &c., the tearing wind making it impossible to go out with any comfort.

Friday, 13th October.
Up to the line again this morning. Our front is very extended, going right down to Bond street, near the Richebourg factory. I did a shoot down by Copse street close there this afternoon and had tea with Bigwood in the company headquarters dugout. The lines are only seventy yards apart just there. I share my mess with some rather delightful little pink nosed mice, one of whom will come on to the table and eat crumbs, sitting up on his hind legs, but he will not feed from my hand, and I have to sit very still while he is there.

Saturday, 14th October.
Ammunition carrying all day. No shooting till 10.0 p.m., when there was a combined artillery and T.M. shoot for half an hour. The Hun was extraordinarily quiet, not answering at all. The men say he keeps a caretaker in the line, with his wife and little boy, the latter firing the very-lights : but the assistance of the lodgers is called in when any real trouble arises.

Sunday, 15th October.
Went over after breakfast to meet Vacher at the top of Hun street to

pick some emplacements on beyond for a little show that is coming off : this took the whole morning. A beautiful sunset. Press, the machine gunner, and I went souveniring among the old Hun trenches behind here, but found nothing better than two 5.9 duds which we left where they were.

Monday, 16th October.
Shoot on at 7 and 8 a.m. Met Thacker at Hun street after breakfast and took him on to Bond street, shewing him round generally. The bit beyond the La Bassée road is in a nasty state : it is now the Huns' favourite spot for his heavy minnies. Thacker did not stop for lunch, so I had mine with A company of the 8th Worcesters. Their headquarters is in the support line near the Bute street dump ; and I had a pleasant lunch with Walford, Constable, and H. L. Evers. Another very cold night.

Tuesday, 17th October.
Vacher relieved me at 11 a.m. Rain in the afternoon and all night.

Wednesday, 18th October—Thursday, 19th October.
Still raining. To the line on Thursday in preparation for a raid which was cancelled. We had some chaff with the 8th Worcs. Bn. Hq. on the way back.

Friday, 20th October.
Again up to the line for lunch, and worked during the afternoon detonating and carrying ammunition. At 9.30 p.m. my old company (B company) of the 8th Worcs. tried a raid on the right of the La Bassée road, protected by our bombardment for which we had eight guns up. They failed to get in, and at about 10.30 the Huns began a little on their own account, mostly with 4.2's on the front line. We got back by midnight. Before the show I saw one or two bright meteors.

Saturday, 21st October.
Saw 4 of Jupiter's satellites through a sniper's telescope.

Sunday, 22nd October.
Evers and Major Griffiths called for me at 10.30 a.m. and we walked into Estaires by the La Bassée road and had lunch. While we were eating at the Hotel de Ville in walked Capt. W. A. Odgers, just back from the Boulogne course, so we sat on some time talking, and then Evers and I went to the piano, where we amused ourselves, finally walking back through Fosse, where we got a tea out of Bomford, the 8th Worcs. transport officer.

Monday, 23rd October.
Up again for my turn in. This time it is a brand new dugout near Mogg's hole, which I share with Thomlinson the machine gunner. Thacker has gone sick, and so Field is in charge of the battery.

Tuesday, 24th October.
Worked all day in the rain placing guns and ammunition for a dummy raid. Cpl. Milliner was killed by a small T.M. near Church street. This is,

I think, the first fatal casualty the battery has had. The 'raid' came off at 8.30 p.m., the Huns keeping very quiet.

Wednesday, 25th October.
Everything is intolerably wet now. Even the new dugout leaks, having a flat roof. The Huns treated us to a little morning hate between 9.30 and 10.30, but did no damage. I got hold of a pair of thigh gum boots to-day which have their uses. A good deal of B lines to the right of Mogg's hole is three feet deep in water.

Orders came at 9 p.m. to fire to-morrow morning at Oxford street with the two guns now at Bond street. These being a mile and a half apart it cannot be done. I sent off a messenger to try and get them up.

Thursday, 26th October.
I met my messenger while on the way up to Church street at 7 a.m., saying he had not been able to find the right hand guns at all. I spent the day wandering up and down the brigade front, very bored, very wet, and very tired.

Friday, 27th October.
I was woken up at 4 a.m. by a heavy bombardment away on the right. At 5 a.m. the right battalion—the 8th Worcs.—rang up for retaliation. I struggled down to Bond street and reached their right company headquarters at 6.30 a.m., by which time all was quiet. I rang up battalion from there to know if they still wanted anything done. They said 'carry on,' so I took up the two guns, which the Worcesters had been unable to find, and fired off fifty rounds. This of course started the whole show over again, but as I had no more ammunition I came away.

During the morning an officer of the 169th L.T.M.B. came up, who is going to take over from us. The Worcesters have rather got the wind up over this business, and so I have to sleep down their end of the sector to be ready in case of need. What I shall do I don't know, as there is no ammunition there to speak of.

I and the relieving officer then went down, in pouring rain of course, to A company's hq. via battalion hq. The company fed and lodged us. I saw Constable there and a new man, Cade by name, said to be a relation of Jack.

Saturday, 28th October.
We were not called up last night fortunately, but went back to our own dugout and then started round the line. Incidentally an amusing thing happened near Mogg's hole. Some R.E.'s took two or three hours with a pump getting three feet of water out of a trench into the ditch beyond the parados. In one hour after they had finished the trench was half full again of water, which was seen bubbling up through a rat hole. I took 169 round. He was immensely surprised at being able to look over the top, which you can do here without much danger.

I left him at 2 p.m. and came out of the line for the last time with an N.C.O. and four men. We went back to the machine gunners' billet, where I had my old bed and dined with B company of the 4th Gloucesters, commanded by Capt. T. S. Foweraker. Now that we are really leaving

this sector I feel quite sorry; since the Neuve Chapelle line in fine weather is not at all bad, and the billets have become a good deal more than mere rest houses.

Sunday, 29th October.
All great things begin on a Sunday. We started our trek down south at 9.0 a.m. and marched to Busnes, through Paradis and Cornet Malo, at which latter place we halted for an hour for lunch. Soon after this we left the Gloucesters and marched some way along the canal bank, reaching the battery in a rather nice billet at 4 p.m. Field and Vacher are alone.

Monday, 30th October.
I have to go on parade from 11-1 and 2-4 training sixteen men of the 6th Gloucesters in Stokes gun work. There is nothing much to do in the town. Saw Clarke, ex-tramways.

Tuesday, 31st October.
Parades again with my sixteen men. Fuller-Maitland's 'Brahms' came to-day, of which I read a good deal in the evening. We have an addition to the mess in M. K. Butler, Brigade Salvage Officer, Middlesex Regiment.

Wednesday, 1st November.
We left Busnes at 11, Thacker turning up just as we were out in the road ready to start, and marched, pushing our handcarts, and without packs, to Auchel, passing through Lillers on the way. Towards the end we came into quite hilly country and saw several big slag heaps. Gen. Mackenzie passed up the column, and said the Huns raided the Red Lamp corner on the night of the relief. I walked round the town with Field when we arrived and had tea. When just getting into the town we were held up by a long procession, almost entirely men, in black clothes, but with the most wonderful ribbons and collars, like masons or oddfellows. They might have had any business from a trade union dispute to a funeral, but were probably keeping Toussaint. In the evening, at Butler's suggestion, we played vingt et un.

Thursday, 2nd November.
We started in the rain at 8.30 a.m. and marched to Orlencourt, lunching off damp sandwiches under a haystack, and getting in at 3 p.m. There was a little difficulty over our billets as a company of 4th Gloucesters had gone into ours. However, we turned them out, and so all was well. I had a most charming little room and bed.

Friday, 3rd November.
I went on in advance on a bicycle to Bailleul aux Cornailles, not very far, and found our billets—a farm at the end of a blind road, about a mile to the south east. It is a great gaunt farm house with stone floors, and the owners made in the same style. We did not make great friends and slept on the stones. In the afternoon Field, Butler, and I went into St. Pol, getting a lift on a lorry. We had tea first, then I had my hair cut,

and we finally met for dinner at the Hotel de France. Butler, who had been over last night, introduced me to the waitress as the Prince de Condé, and Field as the Duc de Vendôme : I forget his own title. We had a very good dinner, got a lift half way back in a staff car, and walked the rest along the railway, singing.

Saturday, 4th November.
On parade to-day with my Gloucester men. This evening I finished my quintet, for which I am very glad.

Sunday, 5th November.
Off at 10.30 a.m. to Ococches, crossing the main road and going on south-west about six miles, in a tearing wind. At the top of the hill between Ligny-St. Flochel and Ternas we got a splendid view, looking north right up to Laventie, I should think, though one could not quite make it out.
Indifferent billets. They all, except me, went into St. Pol again. I went to bed on the floor, and slept.

Monday, 6th November.
Marched to Wavans, on the Auxi-le-Chateau-Doullens road, through Frevent and Bonnières. The last few miles were very tiring as we went by the wrong road, which led us over some very bad country. We got in at 4.0, very tired, and were met by Vacher, who had gone on ahead, saying he had cornered all the eggs in the village. I have a bed in a little room next the mess. The machine gunners are in the village as well as ourselves.

Tuesday, 7th November.
Wet again. Vacher and I walked into Auxi for tea.

Wednesday, 8th November.
Wet. Sent off quintet home by post. Walked with Vacher after lunch to Frohen le Grand to the Field Cashier. After waiting about for an hour or so we were informed that he had run short of money, so we came away saying things about soft jobs in the Army.

Thursday, 9th November.
Wet again. To Auxi for money from some Army school, and again disappointed. We came away, not even getting tea.

Friday, 10th November—Tuesday, 14th November.
Drilled the 6th Gloucesters. Once we had a jolly dinner with the machine gunners, and one day we had chicken for dinner, from this farm. The M.G.'s spent a good deal of time with firing competitions and horse races, which we sometimes watched.

Wednesday, 15th November.
We left Wavans, where we had quite a good time and marched to Le Quesnel farm, four miles west of Doullens. The road was horrible, most of the way, close to the river Authie, a foot deep in mud sometimes, and marked second class on the map, which means volumes. The farm itself and the inhabitants are simply an intensified edition of the one near

Bailleul aux Cornailles, where we were on the third of this month. We slept on stone floors again, and I discovered that I had left my watch behind at Wavans.

Thursday, 16th November.
We left the farm with no regret at 9 a.m. and I entered upon a day of misfortunes. The battery marched to Fransu, north-west of Domart-en-Ponthieu. I rode back on a bicycle to Wavans for my watch. To begin with there was a high wind blowing, which proved to be against me whichever way I went : then the gear wheel of the bicycle sometimes refused to catch in the hub of the back wheel, so that my feet would revolve with lightning-like rapidity and the bicycle stopped. I rode back along the main Auxi-Doullens road. When just east of Frohen I got off to rest and adjust my equipment, and being none too calm in mind, threw my things down peevishly on to the grass by the roadside : then, starting again in five minutes, I unknowingly left a nice map case on the ground containing, among other things, a nice trench map of the whole divisional sector at Laventie. At last I got to Wavans, recovered my watch, and then, not knowing the road, discovered the loss of my map case. I rode back at once to look for it and came to the exact spot where I had halted : however someone else had found it first and appropriated my map case. I rode then back to Wavans again, and by asking my way and taking a sketch off someone else's map on the back of an envelope I started off for Fransu. I was deceived by the map into taking a second class road again, and had to get off and push the bicycle, through St. Acheul to Montigny. There the road became better, and I rode on through Prouville and Ribeaucourt to Fransu, where I met Vacher, who had come on ahead billetting. Our mess was in the curé's house, and I slept there. We all had some food, omelette and potatoes, and bread and jam, at a cottage where the woman was most charming and ready to do all she could for us, in great contrast to the people at Le Quesnel. We had dinner at the mess and the curé introduced himself. He was almost the fattest man I ever saw, and spoke English not quite as well as I do French. However, he had been at a Theological school at Oxford, and so I played that for all it was worth, and by its means got him to allow the servants to sleep in the kitchen, and myself to play on his piano. I had with me the 'Emperor,' and Brahms' B Major trio. So all ended well.

Friday, 17th November.
We left Fransu at 8.30 a.m. and marched with the machine gunners, two of our handcarts tied to each of their limbers, going through Domart-St. Leger and Canaples to La Vicogne, about six miles south of Doullens on the main road. On the way we heard that the 7th Worcesters had been run up to the line in lorries and thrown into an attack. The first part was quite true, but they were not in the show : they went up afterwards to consolidate in front of Thiepval.

Our march was fairly comfortable, except for the cold. There was a bitter wind all the way. I was behind, with Field, and we managed to amuse ourselves. We and the machine gunners were again together

in a big farm. I slept in a loft with three others, getting into pyjamas as usual, in my fleabag. Just before we went to bed it began snowing.

Saturday, 18th November.
We left La Vicogne at 9.0 a.m. and marched "under our own steam" to Warloy, five miles west of Albert. It was frightfully cold, and raining most of the way ; ice on all the ponds, but not much snow about. Adding insult to injury they put us under canvas just outside the village. I was in a tent with Field and Crick, the latter from the 8th Worcesters, attached for instruction with sixteen men. They were most useful in pushing our handcarts ! Field and I struggled out into the village for some food. We went to an inn, but they had nothing except bread and coffee ; so we bought a lot of tinned food at a canteen opposite, and carrying it across, ate it in the warm estaminet with their coffee, and then went to bed. There is a prisoners' camp next to our tents, heavily wired in.

Sunday, 19th November.
We left Warloy fairly late in the morning, and marched to Martinsart, north-west of Albert. The roads are shocking : endless streams of traffic both ways. We marched through Senlis and Bouzincourt. From there to Martinsart we seemed quite to be coming to the war again, every now and then passing groups of Germans, with one English soldier to every twenty-five or thirty, looking on with slung rifle. Some biggish guns here and there confirmed the warlike impression. We reached our billet about 4 p.m. Every few minutes the house is shaken by a 9.2 or 6-inch Naval gun firing from the valley just below.

Monday, 20th November.
In the morning Thacker, Vacher, and I walked up to the ridge east of Mesnil, a village looking almost like Neuve Chapelle, where we had a most striking view over Thiepval and the valley of the Ancre. It was really a most wonderful sight. We could see the shells bursting each side of the river, with an occasional coloured light. As it was only four days since the last big attack here, in which we had taken Beaumont Hamel and pushed on almost to Grandcourt, there was an especial interest in the part we were looking at. There seemed to be a rather unusual amount of "artillery activity." The extraordinary thing was to look on calmly at it all with never a shell near us. A few landed in the valley by the river, but nothing closer. In Thiepval we could not see a single house or wall standing, only the bare stumps of trees where the wood had been, and the ground honeycombed with shell holes, something like a picture of the moon. There was no life at all. One working party of about twenty men going up the slope by Beaumont Hamel was all we saw of movement.

In the afternoon we walked into Albert, on the way seeing three tanks—the first in our experience. Albert is a dull place : hardly any civilians, which is perhaps not surprising ; no shops to speak of, and those extortionate ; and all the streets inches deep in mud.

My impression of the Somme so far is that it is much more like a vast

open-air exhibition than a war. We have had no shells quite near us, and spend our time going about and seeing the most wonderful things.

Tuesday, 21st November.
Foggy morning. Field and I walked down the road to an artillery canteen and bought some food, including a large slab of cake, which I immediately dropped in the mud, amusing Field and the gunners very much. Fortunately the cake was not much damaged. Our cuisine is immensely improved now by a mincer, which opens up limitless possibilities to the cook. On the way back from the gunners' canteen we stopped at a 60-pounder emplacement and had the gun explained to us by a rather nice corporal, who had been there since July 1st.

After lunch Field and I went up to Englebelmer, looking for a 15-inch Naval gun which we were told was there. We did not see it, but saw instead a 15-inch howitzer and a large number of shells. They were not firing to-day, which was a pity, but it was very interesting all the same.

Between 5 and 6 p.m. there was a big bombardment on both sides of the Ancre, all the guns round here firing hard; so Vacher and I toiled up to the Mesnil ridge again to see what we could. It was very hard to make out what was happening. The Huns seemed to send up a large number of red rockets somewhere by Grandcourt, but beyond that we could see little except flashes of bursting shells, in itself a fine sight. It was very cold and rather foggy, and I gave myself a fine cold in consequence.

Wednesday, 22nd November.
The battery moved this morning to Albert. Cpl. Medland and I walked through Aveluy and up Nab road to try and find Mouquet Farm. On the way we passed through the old front line and No Man's land, which was very interesting, and would have been much more so but for the fog, which prevented our seeing more than two hundred yards or so. Presently we came to a gang of men working, and there the road ended abruptly. It is an entirely new one they are making. We found some duckboards and went along on them until I came up with a Capt. J. H. Bevan, whom I had seen before at Frohen le Petit and who was up at the House with me. He is now on this divisional staff. The ground was quite extraordinary; hardly a yard unturned by a shell hole, and some of them six or eight yards across and half full of water. At last we came to the remains of a road, embanked on one side, and on both sides of which was a line of 18-pounder batteries, set close together. There must have been quite an hundred guns in a quarter of a mile. I asked the way and was told to "follow that line of trees and Mouquet farm is that mound on the skyline." The trees were mere stumps of what had been, I suppose, an orchard, as the man said they were apple trees, though I don't know how he knew. There were no duckboards here, so we had to dodge about among the shell holes and artillery aiming marks. The amount of salvage lying about was amazing—rifles, equipment, shell-cases, bombs, everywhere; and close to the farm was a tank stranded in the mud. The farm itself consisted of a mound of bricks and a hole in the ground, out

of which a man in shirt sleeves was looking rather anxiously. They had been shelling the place just before we came up. There was no vestige of a wall anywhere. We did not stay long, and made our way down along some duckboards leading in a different direction to the one we had come. We stopped on the brow of a hill overlooking the farm and ate our lunch. Then on to Tulloch Corner. The fog had lifted a little, which made it easier and pleasanter going. We went down the Ovillers road a little way and then turned on to the Albert-Bapaume road where we caught a lorry into Albert, a most welcome lift, and found the billets after a little wandering—wire beds and a mess, which is not so bad. Bed early.

Thursday, 23rd November.
Not quite up to the mark to-day : stayed in bed till 11.0 a.m. After lunch we did the round of the shops. This place, Albert, is the nastiest I was ever in, mud six inches deep in all the streets, crowds of men and transport everywhere, shops, i.e. little booths or stalls such as you see in a market, putting on 150% to the usual French prices.

We had a poor but expensive dinner at what is called the officers' tea room, and then to bed.

Friday, 24th November.
A cold day. I wrote some letters in the morning. Thacker went on leave, a very good sign. I had a bath, after waiting about forty minutes for it. We dined again at the tea room, to pass the time.

Saturday, 25th November.
Rain all day : everything beastly.

Sunday, 26th November.
Breakfast at 6.45 a.m. by candle light. Then a start at 7.15 a.m. in pelting rain to some ghastly huts near Aveluy. The mud and the cold, combined with the congestion of traffic, made the whole journey of three miles (and lasting three hours) quite appalling. Vacher and I struggled out in the afternoon, when the rain had more or less left off, for a short walk. The hut is not inviting. There are no beds, so we sleep on the floor, and the stove, when it burns at all, fills the room with acrid smoke. One steps outside into a foot of mud.

Monday, 27th November—Wednesday, 29th November.
Cold and rainy. I spent the mornings drilling the attached men. Wednesday Vacher went up to Mouquet to take over from the 184th brigade.

Thursday, 30th November.
Started after lunch to Mouquet with a party of men. We arrived safely without incident. The dugout, a German one, is about twenty feet deep and has several entrances and passages. Our rations went astray so I set out with two men to find them on Nab road. We got there at last, on the way meeting with an artillery sergeant stogged in the mire in a shell hole, and crippled with rheumatism. We hauled him out with some difficulty and passed him on to a doctor. We found our mess stuff

dumped by the side of the road and brought away as much as we could carry. Then Field went down with a party of men for the rest. He could not bring all, and had to leave most of the crockery, &c. We got to bed at 11 p.m., sharing quarters with Lieut. P. P. Perry, in temporary command of the machine gunners. The beds are sloping boards, arranged like berths on a ship. He has the upper one ; Field and I have the lower, partly raised out of a pool of water by four petrol tins. We all have colds.

Friday, 1st December.

Not much sleep, and a cold and foggy morning. I took a party down at 2 p.m. for the rest of our mess stuff on Nab road, but someone else had been there first and helped themselves to all that was worth having. This dugout is a wonderful place. It communicates with brigade, two hundred yards off, by a passage, now blocked up for sanitary reasons.

Saturday, 2nd December.

Not at all well. Both Field and I are in a sorry state, and compare symptoms. The atmosphere down here is not good for one's head. I did a good deal of writing in the morning. After lunch Field went up the line, and I went out along High trench, running east from the farm, and saw some strange sights : rifles with fixed bayonets lying just outside the trench where they had been dropped by our men on one side ; and Hun rifles with, occasionally, their owners, on the other side. I noticed no unburied English there. I find I am getting dreadfully callous, which is, I suppose, inevitable.

Sunday, 3rd December.

Bit of a thaw this morning : not out till after tea, when Field and I took a walk to Rifle dump.

Monday 4th December.

Clear day : aeroplanes out in the morning. Except to go upstairs and look out I did not move, and went to bed early.

Tuesday, 5th December.

Frost again and dull sky. Not out much. The Hun shelled the farm from 2-4 p.m. with about 100 5.9's. His shooting was pretty good too, considering that it was unobserved. He plumped straight for us and for brigade, leaving the hundred and fifty yards in between quite untouched. Towards the end he brought off a lucky one which knocked in our entrance. The shell landed on top of the staircase, leaving the top few steps untouched and the last few. A wooden door at the bottom was blown off its hinges, and all our candles put out. The men had the wind up properly, and so, in fact, did we, though with tremendous savoir faire all Field and I did was to swear simultaneously and ask each other for the matches. Still it was unpleasant : but the closing of that staircase makes our quarters much warmer.

Wednesday, 6th December.

Dull morning. Again the Hun plastered this place from 1.45 to 2.30 p.m. At that time there came a pause, and so Weeks and I scurried out

and got away from the farm as quick as possible on our way to the line via Rifle dump, Zollern trench, and Regina, to our dugout in the Ravine, called by those who know 'Death Valley.' We were not spotted, and, being only two, came through quite safely and easily. The dugout is in the side of a chalk rise and goes down deeper than Mouquet, and with the hill above it makes one feel very safe indeed. The nuisance is having to leave it occasionally. The valley bends round to the left lower down towards Grandcourt, and is under direct observation by the Hun, who slings over a 5.9 or some H.E. shrapnel at parties of more than three. The dugout is more than forty steps down with a passage at the bottom about four feet wide and ten long, containing a seat and dining table. Beyond this is a smallish hole leading to a similar passage and staircase, thus providing an emergency exit. I share our half with the 183rd machine gun officer and his N.C.O.'s and men. Two of the former, Sgt. Daniels and Cpl. Myers, are most entertaining. I slept, or rather lay under the table.

Thursday, 7th December.
A most convenient mist early this morning. I went with Cpl. Chudleigh to the left hand gun on Sunken road, six hundred yards to the left along Regina. On the way back meeting Spooner, the brigadier, with Rabone. I also went a little way down the ravine to see Smith, the machine gunner, in his dugout. I did not go out again. There was a little shelling in the afternoon. The Hun does " vertical searching " up one side of the ravine as far as " second assembly," a trench further up which he is particularly fond of, and where no one lives, and then comes down the other side—5.9's at 20 or 30 yard intervals.

Friday, 8th December.
Spent the night on a petrol tin at the bottom of the stairs, and did not sleep much. We are a bit congested in here. I went to the left gun early, and after lunch took Weeks with me up to the Aid post, where a battalion doctor gave me something for a headache. We had a good deal of shelling after dark, especially away on the left by the next Division's front.

Saturday, 9th December.
Slept quite a good deal. It was raining early and rather clear, so I did not go over to the left. In the afternoon my relieving officer came down, Coates, from 182nd brigade, rather a good fellow, We had our first casualty to-day, one of his runners hit by some H.E. shrapnel through standing too long at the door.

Sunday, 10th December.
A trying day. To begin with I took Coates over to the left gun, and generally showed him round. With our usual luck the day was magnificently clear, so that the Kaiser in Berlin could have had a splendid view of our relief. I made exhaustive arrangements for no more than two men ever to be together, and those at 100 yard intervals. I sent my men one by one into Regina and sat with them there. The Hun was putting 5.9's at minute intervals on to Second Assembly, about two hundred yards beyond, which made a tremendous noise coming straight over our heads,

but did us no harm. One dropped very short, only about fifty yards away, and was rather disturbing. I moved the men up a bit and sent them away two by two at long intervals and waited for 182. They came at last, after what seemed an age, really only about half an hour, in two clumps of eight each : enough to bring down a whole barrage. I explained the situation briefly and suggested they should get into the trench. Then they must needs stand about in a great mob outside the dugout door. However by a miracle the Hun continued his attentions to Second Assembly and let us alone. I settled up with Coates and crawled away with Weeks feeling pretty dead. If I hadn't been so much on edge I might have stopped to look at the view from Zollern trench, which I know was quite worth seeing. However my whole energies were bent on removing myself as quickly as possible. I'm afraid I'm no hero ! They were shelling the tramway so we struck across country to the right, through Zollern redoubt, reaching Mouquet about 1 p.m. Here I had some tea and cake and came straight away with Field on to Nab road. Neither of us could do more than crawl, and the men were in like condition. In Aveluy we put them into a passing lorry, but as there was no room for us we two walked on. We reached the huts at 3 p.m. and got straight into bed. I have hardly ever been more tired.

I seem to have made a good deal of this day, but in truth a relief in such a place is no joke, and on a clear day, coming on top of ten days " in " is no joke at all.

Monday, 11th December.
Not up till midday : somewhat jaded. Field and I walked into Albert and had a very good bath, our only activity. Bed again at 7.30 p.m.

Tuesday, 12th December.
The battery moved to Hedauville. I walked in to Albert and after some time found an R.M.A. workshop, where they unscrewed the base of my Hun aerial torpedo, souvenired from Mouquet farm. I got a lift back and took the H.E. out of my torpedo—curious yellow stuff looking like sandy sugar. At 2 p.m. I started in a lorry which I picked up at Northumberland avenue and went to Hedauville. There I changed and got on another going to Acheux, meeting Bomford at the station, and after an immense wait got into the train at 10. It started at 10.20 p.m. I was travelling with J. F. Bomford, Transport Officer of the 8th Worcs., and G. M. I. Blackburne of the 7th Worcs.

Wednesday, 13th December.
We reached Candas soon after midnight and had to change, walking nearly a mile to the main line station. We were told the train would come in about 6.30 a.m., so we sat in the waiting room, frightfully cold and rather hungry. Blackburne and I ate a tin of pineapple to stave off the pangs. Every now and then we heard a train and rushed out only to see it go by with munitions of some kind. At length someone told us the train had run off the rails ! About 7.30 a.m. Bomford and I walked down the line to get warm and there saw a train standing idle. We climbed up, and asking what it was were told it was the leave train, all

right, but part was off the rails. We got in and sat down, to keep our seats, and presently the train drew in to the station and we were thankful then that we had kept our places. I hopped out and got in the luggage, our two packs, and off we went.

Boulogne at 3 p.m. We went straight to the quay and on to the boat, where we took a cabin in which I washed and shaved. Folkestone 5 p.m., Victoria 7.15 p.m., and England.

II.

Saturday, 23rd December.

Breakfast in the Grosvenor Hotel, Victoria, at 6.15 a.m. There I met Bomford, with whom I had travelled the other way, and his cousin D. R. Bomford, who had been wounded at Richebourg. My pack this time was very heavy, being filled with some extra clothes, &c. The train started just before seven, after prolonged whistling, and a few minutes late, and swung down to Folkestone by 9 a.m. There we found quite a storm on, waves dashing over the platform, and a furious wind. Bomford and I waited on the station some time until we were told the boat was put off till 1.0 p.m. Then we walked into the town, up a very steep set of stairs, into the principal part where the shops are. We ordered some food in the Queen Hotel for 11.30 and then went out shopping. I bought two books and a meat mincer (we had lost ours going into the line at Mouquet). My pack was so full by this time that the mincer had to be tied on outside, and one of the books went into my pocket. We had our food then, and acting on a rumour took the precaution to book a room provisionally. We went down again to the pier and were told that the boat would not sail that day, being given a little ticket each to that effect, signed by the Embarkation Officer, a Guards Major. Bomford and I then hurried back to the Queen to claim our room, and were thankful when we got there that we had booked it, as there was quite a crowd trying to get in. We had a single room with two beds, which was quite good enough. After settling our things we had tea at a rather good shop and then bought tickets for the Mikado. This, coming after a nice dinner in the hotel, was a much better ending to the day than we had expected. There were a good many officers in the theatre, all returning from leave, and also one or two Naval officers, and a large number of wounded soldiers. We went to bed at 11 p.m., hoping the storm would continue.

Sunday, 24th December.

The morning was fine and the wind had died away, so there was no hope. The boat started at 10 a.m., and reached Calais at 12. Boulogne apparently was out of use. On landing Bomford and I spent some time avoiding the R.T.O.'s and such like staff lest we should be put in charge of a party of men. There were no notices up and no directions as to where we should go. At last we found out that the place to go to was the Gare Centrale. An R.T.O. there would have nothing to do with us, and told us to go to Fontinette, about a mile out. About half way there we picked up a tram, but we had hardly sat down in it before the electricity gave

out, and we walked on to the station. There we found an R.T.O. just come from Boulogne. That port, we heard, had been temporarily closed by the Bosche. This R.T.O. knew nothing at all, and had the grace to say so. He thought our train might start the next morning. We went back to the town and engaged the last two rooms at the Hotel Centrale, a great piece of luck. We did not go out again.

Monday, 25th December. Christmas Day.
We had been told to be at Fontinette at 8 a.m. and had asked to be called at 6. I woke up in a panic at 2 a.m., thinking we were late, and was finally woken soon after 6 by Bomford. The hotel people never bothered. We again had to walk most of the way to Fontinette, but found the train, due in at 3 a.m., not yet arrived. There were swarms of men and officers waiting for it, thousands apparently. We found a refreshment hut, run by two ladies, who let us into their own room at the back of the counter, which was besieged by Tommies, and gave us some very nice coffee and bread and butter. Just before that we had some amusement provided by some Irish Fusilier officers fresh from England who had been told to report to someone in authority—the reply was " I know nothing about you and have no instructions ; go away." Rather brutal ; and some disinterested spectator suggested their taking the next boat back. We saw them afterwards on our train. However, while we were still eating in the canteen the train arrived, and we rushed out. It was an immense length, as all these troop trains are here, and there were very few " firsts." We spied one at last and ran alongside it as best we could through the throngs of men. At last it stopped and I climbed up and wrenched open the door just in time to see a gunner officer crawl in through the opposite window. We settled in, three a side, Bomford and I having corners. The others in the carriage were a Capt. Stanley of our divisional A.S.C., two gunner subalterns of the 11th Division, and a subaltern on a 15-inch howitzer, one of those Field and I saw in Englebelmer. They were all very pleasant and cheery, and being in close confinement for some fifteen hours we got to know each other quite well towards the end. The train moved by incredibly slow stages through Boulogne, Etaples, and Abbeville. At Etaples we got out to stretch our legs. A little way down the train some people had got out, kit and all, valises, camp beds, &c., and announced that they were fed up with the journey and had decided to stop there. These casual people are quite amusing. We reached Candas in darkness, at 10 p.m., and changed to the other station, getting to Acheux at 1.0 a.m. As the train could go no further, and was not going back, we stayed in it to sleep till the morning.

Tuesday, 26th December.
We left the train soon after seven and breakfasted in a café in the village. Bomford went off and I shaved in a cottage where a woman gave me some hot water. I presently ' jumped ' a lorry to Northumberland avenue and found the battery in huts near Aveluy wood, where we were before. After lunch I walked out with Vacher to bring back the battery from a fatigue party in the wood.

Wednesday, 27th December.

In the morning Vacher and I walked up to a dugout near Tulloch corner to reconnitre, as we go up to-morrow. I found H. P. Cole there, late of B1 Marlborough, and another man, B. K. Parsons, also a Warwick. We returned by 3 p.m. and went early to bed.

Thursday, 28th December.

Up to Tulloch corner in the morning. I share quarters with Mullet, the brigade bombing officer, and I think an ex-ranker. He is not very amusing. Anyhow he is responsible for all that goes on here, and " took over " everything. I have most of the battery up here, who go on carrying parties to the infantry dumps. I sat in and finished ' The Broad Highway.' The dugout is similar to Mouquet, though fortunately quite dry. Mullet is on top, I underneath.

Friday, 29th December.

Not out much. I sent Weeks into Martinsart for my Green's History, which he did not like doing at all. I read some in the evening.

Saturday, 30th December.

Very wet in the dugout. Last night, after heavy rain, the water came in down the stairs from the trench outside. We cleared a passage for the water to flow away, and made things much better.

Sunday, 31st December.

Read Green all day. I went upstairs at midnight. All our batteries started firing salvoes, and the Hun did a little on his own account, but nothing very much. I heard that on Christmas Day the only firing done was one round from every gun on the Corps front at noon.

Monday, 1st January—Friday, 5th January, 1917.

Not much to relate. The weather was cold and wet. On Thursday the Hun put down a lot of tear gas shells into our valley and shelled the batteries in front. We sat up in our gas helmets for about an hour, weeping copiously.

Saturday, 6th January.

About midday we were relieved by 182, for which I was very thankful. Nine days in such a position is apt to become boring. I left about 1.30 p.m. with the last of my men and reached the huts by 3 p.m. Here I found beds, a great addition to comfort. We have staying with us Colin Coates of 182nd T.M.B., waiting to go on leave.

Sunday, 7th January.

I got up at 12 and went a walk with Coates to Crucifix corner, where he saw his O.C.—G. W. Hopkins, of Cotton House, Marlborough. Then we went on up the Authuille road past the salvage dump, where Coates collected one or two souvenirs. We went on through Authuille, crossed the river, and came back to the huts through the wood.

Rain began about six. We are sleeping to-night without valises as Thacker thinks we shouldn't be packed up in time.

Note.—I give here a list of the battery who were up with me at Tulloch corner.

Sgt.	Williams	L.-Cpl.	Impey	L.-Cpl.	Wilmot
Cpl.	Eves	Pte.	Allen, J.	Pte.	Clarke (runner)
	Guest		Allen, G.		Massey
	Hunt		Archer		Honeysett
(,,	Medland)	Cpl.	Mitchelmore		Green
L.-Cpl.	Hingley	L.-Cpl.	Walters		Jones
Cpl.	Chudleigh				
Pte.	Dingle	Pte.	Hughes	Pte.	Norwood
	Bowater		Jennings		Taylor
	Bolton		King		Britton
	Donovan		Long		Short
	Guest, S.		Scadding		Price
	Hackett		Bowen		Brotherton
	Andrews				

Monday, 8th January.
Coates went off early on some job for his brigade. We all got up at owl's light, in fact. Vacher went off with the battery and I stayed to hand over the billets, which is infinitely preferable to marching with the men. The 184th brigade man came along about 11 a.m. and I walked up to Martinsart to see if the stores had been handed over by the corporal. Coming down again I had a bad moment or two when I discovered I was not wearing my signet ring. However I found it soon in a pocket, where I had put it before washing in the morning. I got a lorry to Hedauville, and just caught up the battery there. We were billeted in the village, with wire beds and a good mess.

Tuesday, 9th January.
Had breakfast in bed this morning. Rather a wet day. My trench boots have come and are rather a success. In the afternoon I went for part of the time to watch Vacher playing soccer. He was playing for a divisional school to which he has been lately on a course. After tea I wrote letters, including one to Morshead, of whom I heard from Brent. Smith while on leave. A heavy bombardment this evening. They say the 11th Division are going over from the Hansa line, but I don't know if that is true.

Wednesday, 10th January.
Rather cold to-day. I have a crowd of 6th Gloucesters to teach, including an officer, one Skey, who comes from Malvern and is an organist. I discovered this by accident in the mess. I was whistling a tune from a Beethoven piano sonata and he followed it up by whistling the next movement : rather surprising. He has been to Worcester and heard Atkins play, &c.

Thursday, 11th January, and Friday, 12th January.
Cold and wet. Gun drill with the attached men.

Saturday, 13th January.
Very cold : a little rain. I walked into Acheux in the afternoon and bought an acetylene lamp. Our expenditure of candles is so enormous nowadays that we think this will economise, especially as carbide is an Army issue. I came back to find Evers seated up at tea, come over for a meeting of some kind from Varennes, where the 8th Worcesters are. We spent the rest of the evening trying to make the lamp light.

HEDAUVILLE—ARGENVILLERS

Sunday, 14th January.
Slack day. Over to Varennes in the afternoon to see the 8th Worcs. Roads very bad and muddy. I saw several people I knew and had tea at the headquarter's mess, coming back at 6.0 p.m. for a meeting, presided over by Neville Talbot, who is 5th Army Headquarter's Chaplain, on the National Movement for Repentance, as applied to the Army.

Monday, 15th January.
Nothing to say.

Tuesday, 16th January.
We left Hedauville at 9.0 a.m. and marched to Beauquesne. We have no handcarts now, and so we are marching in full pack for the first time since I left the battalion. Thacker has been wanting to get rid of them, but I like marching easily and " straggling all over the road " as he says. However there was a bit of a frost, enough to harden the mud, and the sun was out, altogether making a perfect day of it. We came along very comfortably, getting in at 6.0 p.m. Vacher and I are in the same house as the mess, with beds and sheets : a great luxury. I went round in the evening with Skey, who is marching with us, to the A.S.C. mess, where I asked Stanley to try and get me a fur coat.

Wednesday, 17th January.
The battery left at about 9 a.m. I stayed behind with six men to clean up billets. Another hard frost has made the roads like glass, and not too easy going, especially for horse transport. I set out at 11 a.m., and after a mile or so stopped a lorry on which I mounted, with my little band. We moved along very well, passing a lot of transport going both ways. The column going our way was some five miles long. We overtook the battery at about a mile on the near side of Candas. There the lorry stopped, so we got out and waited for the others to come up, marching on with them through Bernaville to le Meillard. Billets here seemed scarce. Vacher and I shared a cupboard, he on the bed, I on the floor, able to get in by sleeping diagonally from corner to corner.

Thursday, 18th January.
We stayed in bed till lunch time at midday mainly because we were lazy, and then started for Prouville, four miles away. For some reason I was very tired and it seemed the longest four miles I ever tramped. The country was covered in snow and very desolate looking and it snowed all the way along. However I had quite a good room when we got there, winning the toss with Skey for the bed.

Friday, 19th January.
We left Prouville, an unsatisfactory place, at 9.10 a.m., and marched about ten miles to Hellencourt farm, two miles beyond Gapennes and about six from the village of Crécy. We arrived at 3 p.m. and established ourselves in what promised to be a very good billet. At 5.0 p.m. some officers and men of the 184th Brigade turned up and claimed the place, and so, after appealing to our own brigade about it, we had to turn out and march down to Argenvillers, where we were put into huts totally

devoid of furniture and bitterly cold. There was no means of getting any hot food so we ate some bully beef, and crept into our fleabags. Field had joined us the day before from a course at the 5th Army School and regaled us with stories and songs gleaned there. One verse of what seemed a most promising song I remember, which he sang in a very mournful voice. It was—

> Watching the trains come in,
> Watching the trains come in,
> We sit and hold each other's hand
> As only lovers understand;
> Watching the trains come in,
> Hearing the porters shout.
> As soon as we've watched all the trains come in
> We watch all the trains go out.

Saturday, 20th January.
I managed to keep fairly warm at night and slept long, though it was on the bare boards. I got up late, a rather trying process, and went to an estaminet near, where I had a good breakfast of two fried eggs and coffee. It is to be noticed, though perhaps not surprising, that the farther you go from the line the nicer the French people become. After my food I found the others and we walked out about a mile along the road to a monument which I thought might have something to do with the battle of Crécy, but it turned out to be an ordinary wayside shrine. We all lunched together in the estaminet. Then, not without some search, we found a house for our mess, with a nice woman there and her son. The room is small, about ten feet square, and has five doors. We dined at 6.30 p.m. and retired soon afterwards.

Sunday, 21st January.
Spent a quiet morning. In the afternoon I walked into Abbeville, about six miles, with Thacker and Skey, in my trench boots, a proceeding of which I repented by the time I had got there. The town is good, by far the best we have come across; better than St. Pol, even. We had tea at a good shop, after waiting a little time, as it was very crowded. Then after a little shopping we walked back. I had large blisters on both feet. Except Vacher and myself, all the others have found somewhere else to sleep.

Monday, 22nd January—Tuesday, 23rd January.
Parades and walks. Frost still holding.

Wednesday, 24th January.
I rode in to Abbeville after lunch on a bicycle, and left it at an estaminet near the station. I had tea at a small shop, which was made rather amusing by the comments in English on two French girls and their lap dog by two officers : the girls obviously not understanding a word of what was said. After tea I got some money from the Field Cashier and bought the missing link for our mincer, which has never really worked properly. I dropped it in the returning leave train and scattered the parts all over the carriage and cannot have picked them all up. I also had a most luxurious and delightful hair cut, shampoo, and shave, and then rode back.

Thursday, 25th January—Friday, 26th January.
  Still very cold. Nothing of interest to record.

Saturday, 27th January.
  To Abbeville again on a bicycle, where I bought a cauliflower, as we never get fresh vegetables. I also bought the "Letters of a Temporary Gentleman in France"—a good book—and had, at the Officers' Club, the best bath I've had out here. This evening Vacher and I had a fire in the hut, Selby, his servant, having secured a stove. We also have a bed each, and lie under a mountain of blankets and coats and still shiver.

Sunday, 28th January—Saturday, 3rd February.
  Very cold. Parades as usual.

Sunday, 4th February.
  We moved from Argenvillers to Bussus Bussue, passing through St. Riquier on the way, when we caught a glimpse of a most wonderful west front to the church. The road was very poor, but we arrived at last, and at once went out to secure all the eggs in the village, a most necessary precaution. Vacher and I sleep at the curé's house, in separate bedrooms, with beds and sheets. My bedroom window has hoar frost half an inch thick on it, inside, so I wonder what it will be like at night.

Monday, 5th February—Tuesday, 6th February.
  Going to bed is rather trying, and shaving and washing in the morning. All the hot water I get is heated by my own tommy cooker. There was nothing much to do by day. The men cleaned up, and one day we found a secluded spot and slid on the ice, which is some six inches thick.

Wednesday, 7th February.
  Saw in the paper O. F. Morshead's investiture (M.C.). After lunch Vacher and I went to see a game of soccer between the battery and one of the battalions near, and on the way met Field, just come off leave.

Thursday, 8th February.
  Parade in the morning. In the afternoon I finished the first volume of Mignet's French Revolution in French : rather an effort.

Friday, 9th February.
  Drill all the morning. After lunch I walked into St. Riquier, where I had a look at the church. There is some very interesting carving inside as well as out. Then I went on to see Evers, instructing on a corps sniping school close by. He gave me tea, and I walked back.

Saturday, 10th February.
  A delightful, almost spring-like day. In the afternoon I went out in my trench coat with Vacher, and lay on a grass bank reading.

Sunday, 11th February.
  I heard from Morshead, who described himself as being "between the Tête de Boeuf and the Godbert." In the afternoon I walked with Thacker to Ailly, where brigade is, and sent off a parcel.

1917

Monday, 12th February—Tuesday, 13th February.
Not much to do. I rather stupid with a cold.

Wednesday, 14th February.
We left Bussus regretfully at 11 a.m. and marched behind the 4th Gloucesters to Pont Remy, near Abbeville. Field had gone on ahead to see about the entraining, and told us on arrival that the train would be at least four hours late, and so it was. After a long cold wait we got in at 8.0 p.m. and jolted along through Amiens, reaching Marcelcave at 2 a.m. Here we detrained with some difficulty, having to lift out our handcarts and fix on the wheels, removed for the journey. In the course of the struggle my revolver must have dropped off my equipment, as I never saw it again.

Thursday, 15th February.
After detraining we marched, half asleep, to Wiencourt, and billeted, the men in fairly good quarters, we, all four of us, in one room ten feet by six. Thacker and Vacher went on about 6.0 a.m. in a bus to the line, as we are taking over from the French. Field and I stayed in our beds on the floor till about 11.30, and then went out a little, calling on the machine gunners near by. The owneress of this billet is very nice, and has a pleasant son of about sixteen. She saw some English soldiers marching past the window and said to us, " Les Anglais—toujours ils sifflent " : which is quite true, though I had not thought of it.

Friday, 16th February.
Field went on ahead billeting. We marched at 3.30 p.m. to Framerville, arriving at 6.0 p.m. The place is bare of inhabitants, and in condition rather like Martinsart, that is to say most of the houses are standing but all are knocked about a little. Wire beds.

Saturday, 17th February.
We moved up in the morning to Vermandovillers, through Herleville. There is nothing left here but part of one wall of the church : shell holes everywhere, almost like Mouquet. It was behind the German lines in July last. We are in a very good dugout under an avenue leading to the church. It is made on two levels, the mess, about five feet down, with fallen trees as head cover, and the bedroom, another ten steps or so below that. Vacher is up the line. The French were there when we arrived and cleared out by 3 p.m. There are some enormous shell holes near here, perhaps explained by the fact that our dugout is part of an old German whizz-bang position. We all put on pyjamas at night, Thacker in a bed by himself, Field and I in berths, I on top.

Sunday, 18th February.
In these deep dugouts absence of daylight leads to over-sleeping. Consequently we had breakfast in bed and got up at 12. At 2.0 p.m. I went up the line with Thacker to Ablaincourt, two miles away in a trench, called the Serpentine. It was very muddy, as at last the frost is going. For the first time we are in real trenches, as opposed to breast works at Laventie, and nothing or shell holes on the Somme. We saw Vacher,

in a rather uncomfortable dugout, similar to the one in Regina, and then came away: the whole journey being a rather fatiguing process.

Monday, 19th February.

I spent the morning with Weeks altering my bed, making it into one wide one from two narrow ones, and widening the available dressing space. In the afternoon I went out by myself fixing the position of the tram line on my map by taking bearings on different objects. I made a mistake by taking a bearing on the wrong one of two woods, the other having been almost completely obliterated, so that I had not noticed it.

Tuesday, 20th February.

I went out with Thacker in the morning and finished the tram line. I like that sort of work. The mud now is very bad, and it is preferable to go over the top than in the trench in most places. In the afternoon I went over to see the machine gunners.

Wednesday 21st February.

Field up to the line to-day to take over from Vacher. A nice day with a little sun. I sat out near the dugout with a book. Things seem very quiet here considering there has been an advance fairly recently.

Thursday, 22nd February.

We came out this morning quite easily, with our handcarts, getting back to Framerville about 2 p.m. Bed on the floor again. On the way we passed some of the infantry, stragglers from last night's relief, having been stogged in the Serpentine, which is now waist deep in porridge. They were plastered from head to foot with mud—faces, hands, rifles, everything—and all completely worn out.

Friday, 23rd February.

I stayed in bed very late. Field arrived about 10 a.m. absolutely played out. He took seven hours to come down the Serpentine last night and slept in our dugout up in Vermandovillers. We dined at brigade rear headquarters, where were Mortimer, Bernheim, and one or two more; none of the 'G. side.'

Saturday, 24th February.

Easy day. Field and I went round to see the boss, Raymond, the machine gunners' transport officer, who has just been laid up with a fairly bad go of malaria.

Sunday, 25th February.

Field and I to an early Celebration. I not quite up to the mark. The weather has turned very cold again. After lunch Field and I walked down to Vauvillers, about a mile away, for billets, the battery following on. He and I share a room across the road from the mess. The beds are good, and there is room to move about, and tables for one's things.

Monday, 26th February.

Lovely day. Spent the morning writing letters to Mr. Ruffer, to ask him to get me a new revolver, to Adamson, Oxford, for a new tunic, as

mine are really getting too bad, even for the line, to Charles Fulford, and to Langley, about my quintet. In the afternoon I went a walk by myself towards Lihons.

Tuesday, 27th February.
We heard quite a strafe going on opposite here last night. This morning a paper came through from 5th Army giving prisoners' statements that the Huns will withdraw nearly to Cambrai by the 24th of next month, to their far-famed Hindenburg line. In the afternoon I went out with Field.

Wednesday, 28th February.
Field and I on parade this morning. During an 'easy' he challenged me to race to a tree about three hundred yards away, which I was foolish enough to accept. We were both speechless for about ten minutes afterwards: I hadn't run so fast for years. Thacker met us when we came back with the news that Field was nominated as an instructor in IVth Corps T.M. School. I am very sorry he is going as we are just beginning to know one another, after living for six months cheek by jowl.

Thursday, 1st March.
Field's appointment prompted me to make some enquiries about my own transfer to the M.G.C. which I put in some months ago. However I could get nothing out of anyone. Thacker and Vacher went to the Frolics—the divisional concert party—at Harbonnières, Field and I staying at home.

Friday, 2nd March.
Thacker came into our room at 8.30 a.m. to say Field's job is cancelled. They do enjoy muddling things. He and I went to the Frolics in the evening and sat in the front row with some G staff on our left and old Col. Singleton and some more Q on the right. This was noticed by Capt. Hawkins, a Warwick, and leader of the troupe. He pointed at us saying, "Ah, blue on the right, red on the left, and the soldiers in between." The first time I've ever been called a soldier.

Saturday, 3rd March.
At 9 a.m. the whole battery started in three lorries to go to Vaux-en-Amienois, 4th Army T.M. School, for a course. We went down through Rosières and Caix, on the way passing the 105th Brigade (Cheshires), whom I must go and see when we get back. Beyond Caix we passed a Rupert (observation balloon) and at that moment saw a couple of salvoes of 5.9's land quite close to its base. We passed through Amiens and reached the school about 4.0 p.m. To my astonishment I found the adjutant was J. F. L. Fison, a House man, and contemporary with me. We saw to our billets and then went straight back to Amiens in the same lorry that brought us. We dined at a small place Field knew of, Les Huitres, in a side street of the still more remarkable name "Rue Corps nuds sans testes," having quite a good feed, though somewhat unpretentious, and came back in a lorry about 10 p.m.

Sunday, 4th March.

Parade at 9 a.m. For meals we all sit together at a small table, which is nice in some ways, though you don't get to know other people so well, that way. Six hours gun drill was our start. We have two good sergeant instructors, under a Capt. Peach, from the K.R.R.'s.

Monday, 5th March—Tuesday, 6th March.

Parades and lectures nearly all day, not leaving much time for anything else. Field and Vacher play bridge in the evening, while I look on, or read. Tuesday we had some snow.

Wednesday, 7th March.

I was orderly officer. At 9.0 a.m. I started in a car to get money from the Field Cashier, picking up two officers from the artillery school in this village, one the doctor, who sat in front and was a captain, the other a very young looking subaltern, by name Maxwell, in the 8th Division. We went first to Villers Bretonneux and got the money. Then back through Corbie, where there is another fine façade, to Amiens. Here we stopped for an hour as the doctor wished to do some shopping, and Maxwell and I had lunch at the Godbert, where I saw Tommy, of the machine gunners, come in by train for the day. We had an excellent lunch and returned to Vaux by 4 p.m. A most delightful way of spending the day.

Thursday, 8th March—Monday, 12th March.

Not very well. Snow again, and very cold. Friday we had a big tactical scheme, Stokes, mediums, and heavies all firing live stuff, and the Army Commander, Gen. Rawlinson, watching. I had no job on and so watched too, from a hill at the side. Sunday, Field, Vacher and I had a large dinner at the Huitres, having fortified ourselves with cocktails first at a place near. I met there Cunningham (Nuncle) of the 16th Cheshires. He had heard that we were all killed on July 19th last year. We managed to 'jump' a lorry back to the school.

Tuesday, 13th March.

We left Vaux at 9.0 a.m. in lorries and stopped at Amiens two hours for lunch. Thacker and I went on again in a lorry, Vacher and Field with half the men staying behind and coming on later by train. We went through Moreuil, Quesnel and Rosières to Framerville, getting in at 7 p.m., the same billets as before. We were given a dinner at brigade. The others came along about 9 p.m.

Wednesday, 14th March.

Nothing to do all the morning. We started at 4.30 p.m. for Vermandovillers, arriving at 7, and are in the same dugout, that is Field, Vacher, and I : Thacker sleeps across the way. No one goes up the line now, except for a show : a very nice arrangement.

Thursday, 15th March.

The other three went up to the line looking for emplacements. I spent the morning getting material from the R.E.'s. By tea time the morning positions were cancelled, so Field and I started up at 6.30 p.m. with a

couple of N.C.O.'s to look for some more, on the right of Kratz wood. We went up on the top all the way, because of the mud, and walked along behind the front line. The Hun was very quiet, but once or twice he dropped Very lights fairly close to us, and we had to stand pretty still. We got back at 10 p.m.

Friday, 16th March.
Gentle morning. After lunch I went over to brigade with Field to see R. W. Stevenson, the Staff Captain, about our respective transfers. He told us it was " no use stirring up the mud " at the War Office. At 6.30 p.m. I went up with Vacher to dig the emplacements Field and I had sited last night. There was a good deal doing in one way and another. To begin with I lost my way. It is amazingly hard to find one's way about a place one has only seen in the dark. And most trenches look fairly alike even if you see them before you fall into them. Then, just as we were within twenty yards of the front line, an infantryman on a carrying party just in front of me shot himself in the foot—the most palpable " self inflicted " I ever saw. We then proceeded to dig our emplacements. They were shelling quite a good deal, at any rate much above normal, and landed one or two 5.9's unpleasantly close, from an enfilade gun, I think. We finished in good time, by about 11 o'clock, and had one more sensation on the way back, between Verdun post and the road. Suddenly the Hun sent over about sixteen light shells, about 13-pounders, absolutely on top of us as we were going up the railway : not a shell more than twenty yards away. Quite extraordinarily no one was hit, but it was a near thing. If they had been 5.9's it would have been another story.

Saturday, 17th March.
Vacher, Field and I played bridge in the morning. I am learning the game, and get heavily called over the coals for my mistakes. Field and I went to the Staff Captain's office again, about 12, as I wanted to look up Bingham's address and rank in the Army list. I was going to ask him to interest himself in Field's application for the Indian Army. While we were there a clerk came in, and recognising Field, said : " You're in luck's way, sir ; you have to report at the India Office at once. A letter came through this morning." He was simply beside himself with joy. Then, to cap that, on getting back to the dugout we saw the General (Spooner) talking to Thacker, and he told us that the Huns have evacuated their line—were doing so, in fact, while Vacher and I were digging last night—and our patrols have been up into Chaulnes : which of course knocks our show on the head. Field packed up and left at 6.30. I walked down the Herleville road a little way with him—the second time we have said farewell to each other.

Sunday 18th March.
Nice day. We made preparations to move, and sent some of our kit back, but not our valises. I did some work for Stevenson in the morning, conducting some mules overland, across the Serpentine to right battalion headquarters, where I saw Ball, late of the 8th Worcesters. We left our dugout at 3 p.m. and moved down the Chaulnes road, bivouacking on

the edge of Hart copse. The infantry have gone on about four miles, I believe, and there is a cavalry screen in front of them. We ourselves do things in a more leisurely way and have advanced about one mile only, being still behind our old front line. Weeks and I spent the afternoon making a shelter out of dead branches, &c. I got into pyjamas and was fairly warm. Oddly enough it did not rain.

Monday, 19th March.
A cold wind all day. I walked up into Chaulnes in the afternoon. It is most strange to be walking over places where the Huns have been so recently. Chaulnes wood is in a nasty mess. After tea I hunted about for a dugout to sleep in, and found one in a trench close by at about 7 o'clock, just in the nick of time for the rain came on before I had had all my things moved. Vacher was heroic and choose to stay out, a proceeding of which he repented before dawn came, and actually packed up, but could not find the dugout in the dark.

Tuesday, 20th March.
We breakfasted at 7 a.m. out of doors. It began to snow in the middle of the meal and was piercingly cold, and made me feel rather ill. I did not go out much and went early to bed, a wire one and quite comfortable. Vacher amused us by caricaturing a story in some magazine about a certain fictitious Lady Cheltenham.

Wednesday, 21st March.
Cold day. Thacker and I walked in to Framerville, getting a lift part of the way in a Railway Construction Officer's car. That is the job I should like, nice and safe ; though I suppose even they get run over by their own trains sometimes. We had lunch at brigade and came back, bringing the letters and some mess stuff.

Thursday, 22nd March.
We left the dugout at 3 p.m. and marched with our handcarts through Chaulnes and Pertain to Dreslincourt. In Chaulnes we passed a field kitchen with three dirty mugs on a board. The cook, in a most professional voice, was calling out " Ice cream, a penny, ice cream." I think he must have done it before. The Huns had blown up the road in one place, where it was sunken, and we had to make an excursion into a field. In Dreslincourt it began to snow, and there we turned aside to Dreslincourt wood, where we found a battery position with some excellent dugouts. I found a German comic Army paper, and a rather nice coloured print of a child, apparently unfinished, which I took away. We had been warned against time fuses, &c., and in the night I thought I heard something ticking, which might have been a timed bomb. It turned out to be Vacher snoring, after I had had one or two anxious moments with strained ears.

Friday, 23rd March.
Nice cold day. In the afternoon I went to tea with the 8th Worcesters headquarter's mess in the village, and had a walk afterwards with Evers. It seems we are living in the battery position of a 5.9 gun, not how., which

used to fire at Kratz wood, and P. C. Lyautey, &c., and Col. Bilton shewed me a map with all the targets marked. They are living in the battery commander's billet.

Saturday, 24th March.
In the morning we moved to Bethencourt, on the Somme. This is the first time we have been so close to it, except at Abbeville and Amiens. On the way we passed some of the enormous German sign posts, eliminating any possibility of mistake in your direction : NACH POTTE in letters two feet high carries conviction. Bethencourt has been totally destroyed. As a rule the Hun seems to have put a charge in the cellar and razed the whole house that way. Our headquarters are in the only remaining half of a house in the place. There is a room for a mess, which does duty also for a kitchen, and two bedrooms, with beds souvenired from outside, and a table or two from the house itself.

We had the miserable side of war brought home to us very forcibly this afternoon when a woman came over from Nesle, where all the civilians have been concentrated, and began to dig in a garden near, unearthing a small heap of spoons and forks, and in another place some crockery, hidden from the thievish Bosche.

While at our dinner we were told we must move our quarters to-morrow to make room for a battalion headquarters, which is most annoying.

Sunday, 25th March.
After some search we found a cellar a little way down the street on the other side into which we moved, taking with us most of the furniture, including my bed and a washing stand or dressing table, and a mess table. This manœuvre was performed under the nose of the officer sent to take over.

Vacher and I spent a most wonderfully amusing hour or so watching the R.E.'s building a girder bridge over the river. The personnel engaged seemed to consist almost exclusively of subalterns and sergeant majors, who all gave orders all the time to the confusion of the one or two odd privates who were doing the work. The whole thing, including a man sitting on the top of a derrick trying to untwist some ropes, was very like one of Beuttler's drawings in the Bystander of unrecorded incidents at sea. Altogether a very excellent substitute for a pantomime. The Padre came to tea and afterwards held a service for the men to which I did not go. They always sing such a large number of hymns.

Monday, 26th March.
Rainy. I went out after lunch to the men, who were helping to fill in a large crater blown at a cross roads beyond Croix Molignaux. There were some 4th Gloucesters there and a rather nice subaltern, Crowe, whom I haven't met before. We got back by 7 p.m.

Tuesday, 27th March.
Nothing much to do. The men were out again, but I did not have to go this time. To our great astonishment, while we were at tea, who should walk in but Field. The Indian Army would have none of him

because of his eyes, for which I am not sorry. In the evening we went a walk along the canal, and Vacher nearly fell in, trying to sail about on bits of a wooden bridge the Hun had destroyed.

Wednesday, 28th March.
At 11 o'clock Field and I started on ahead of the battery to find billets in Monchy Lagache, about six miles off. The second village we passed was called Y, just that single letter. It was pretty warm walking, but we had a bottle of Graves on the way, which he had brought from Amiens and which was of great assistance. Thacker came along a little later, and finally the battery, about midnight in a heavy sleet storm. We have an extra officer now from the 4th Gloucesters, Sleap by name. We all were crowded in together in one room, and the men in a big cellar.

Thursday, 29th March.
Men working on the roads all day, clearing up the debris of fallen houses. We moved our billets to a couple of cellars nearer the men : Thacker and Field in one, Vacher, Sleap and I in the other. I have a kind of a bed which is better than the floor at any time. We are extraordinarily lucky compared with the infantry. I have not slept in my clothes since the tour in at Tulloch corner, pyjamas every night ; and I know some of the infantry haven't seen their valises for three weeks. But even they think it a better life than sitting up two hundred yards from the Hun and having bits of old iron thrown at them.

Friday, 30th March.
Wet day, and a strong wind. After lunch Field and I walked over to Croix Molignaux to Dados for some stores. We played four handed bridge in the evening, after dinner.

Saturday, 31st March.
I was on a working party from 8.30 to 1 with the men, carting timber at Trefcon, where I again had a chat with Crowe of the 4th Gloucesters. It was a thoroughly April day, showers of sleet and snow with intervals of sunshine all day. I wrote letters in the afternoon and played bridge in the evening.

Palm Sunday, 1st April.
Had breakfast in bed. Wrote letters and played bridge.

Monday, 2nd April.
We moved at the grizzly hour of 4 a.m. to Villevecque, going by a beautiful road through a sort of park, with the Chateau of Caulaincourt, now a large heap of bricks, on the other side of an ornamental lake. We came to the end of our march about 11.0 a.m. and had to bivouac. The weather was fairly fine, with a high wind. The men made little holes for themselves and we crept in behind a long brick wall with several gaps in it, and made two pseudo-shelters, one for Thacker and Sleap, and one for the rest of us—a most satisfactory arrangement. Rain came on late at night.

Tuesday, 3rd April.
We spent most of the day building a house of the very scantiest materials —about fifty sandbags, some tarred felting, not much though, and stakes which we cut for ourselves. Soon after lunch Field made a bad shot with an axe and smashed the top of his left thumb badly. I went up with him to the doctor, where he nearly fainted. We managed to finish the house, and he went to bed.

Wednesday, 4th April.
A most horrible day—driving snow and sleet all the time. I was out with a working party on a crater from 8.30 to 12.30 and was nearly frozen. I met Edge of the 8th Worcesters and said how beastly it was. His only answer was, " Yes, but thank God they're not shelling." Sleap took on duty after lunch and I went back and played three-handed bridge with Field in bed and Vacher. I got into bed too, as being the most comfortable place.

Thursday, 5th April.
Nice day. At 3 p.m. Thacker, Vacher and I went up to St. Quentin wood, through Marteville, to do a show. I stupidly took no coat, for which I was very sorry later on. We stopped at a battalion headquarters near the Keeper's house, and then, at 8.30, moved up to a quarry just below Fresnoy-le-Petit, our objective. We had brought two guns. Wardrop, the machine gunner, stopped half a mile short and did enfilade fire on to the village from a hill. The infantry went up twice and failed to get in, as there was a good deal of wire, and the Huns in fairly strong force. We stayed till about 3 a.m. and then Thacker and I came back with half the men, getting in at about 6 a.m. On the way Thacker fell asleep during a ten minute halt on the roadside, near Marteville.

Good Friday, 6th April.
Rather a headache, and feeling generally beastly. Thacker went off on his second leave at midday. Sleap went up to join Vacher, whom we had left in front of Fresnoy ; and Field and I moved into Thacker's hut, which was rather better than ours. Very wet night.

Saturday, 7th April.
Vacher came down at 6 a.m., having done a shoot at the village. Some-one from 182nd Brigade came up in the morning to take over, and Vacher went on ahead with the battery to Merancourt, across the river from Monchy Lagache. Field and I stayed on to wait for Sleap, who did not arrive till 1 a.m. We got off then, and arrived at the billets at 3 a.m. Not a bad cellar, but I could not sleep for some reason.

Easter Day, 8th April.
Up by nine. Field and I went up to the village to have his hand dressed, a rather painful operation. We asked about a Service, were told of one, went to look, and found no one there. It was a charming day, and we sat out in the garden at the back of the billet, on a lawn, and had tea. Field has a deck chair he souvenired in Monchy, and I had a chair I found close by.

Monday, 9th April.
Vacher went on ahead in the morning and we followed with the battery at 2 p.m. to Fourques, not very far, and not bad billets. Field and I sleep in a cellar together, but the mess is above ground. News came in of a big show up at Arras.

Tuesday, 10th April—Wednesday, 11th April.
Not very well, and did not emerge much. Snow again both days.

Thursday, 12th April.
Up at 4 a.m. and in the machine gunners mess cart to Nesle with Weeks. From there train to Amiens. It was very wonderful passing the old front line, near Chaulnes and Rosières. We reached Amiens at 3 p.m., and I spent an hour there, managing to cash a cheque for two hundred francs, a most useful piece of work. I left my valise in the station and went to Vaux—4th Army T.M. School, where we were a month ago—in a lorry. On arrival I saw Fison, the adjutant, and persuaded him to let me go back to Amiens in the commandant's car for my kit. While there I had a comfortable dinner at Les Huitres and provided the means for the chauffeur to do the same elsewhere. I share a bedroom in the annexe with one other. Not so bad.

Friday, 13th April—Wednesday, 18th April.
Worked fairly hard on the course. I am on the instruction squad with quite an interesting, amusing, set : " Gallipoli Bill," " Canada," a rampant red headed Canadian in the Durham L.I.; " Chelsea Bill," a Grenadier Guardsman, by name Rolfe ; " Jock," a Scot of course ; and " Guards," a Coldstreamer, by name Bonvalot.
Sunday afternoon (15th) I went into Amiens with Rolfe, the Grenadier, a very tall man, in Fisher Rowe's company. I had a bath and an hair cut, and we both dined at the Godbert. We had a lift back part way in a rather crazy little Flying Corps car, driven by a Canadian, who said he would have gone across the fields if it had been daylight. He nearly did so as it was, once or twice. Tuesday evening I had a delightful treat in the lecture hut of the school, where there is a piano. Bonvalot, the Coldstreamer, played on a violin beautifully, chiefly a sonata by Lekeu, with a very good slow movement. His accompanist was one Stevenson, who had taken his Mus. Bac. from Keble the year I went up.

Thursday, 19th April.
I was rash enough to walk into Amiens with Menny (16th Cheshires, 105th Brigade) and Rose (1st Worcesters), both nice fellows. We did some shopping, dined at the Huitres, and came away in a Flying Corps tender.

Friday, 20th April.
A big live ammunition scheme on in the afternoon, with a bevy of Generals looking on. I was O.C. Brigade dump and had next to nothing to do. There was a very ordinary kind of concert in the evening, followed by a rather amusing ' free night ' in the mess ; everyone very benevolent.

Saturday, 21st April.

A half holiday. The school provided a lorry into Amiens. I bought a new cap, some gloves, and a tie, and also a new fountain pen, having smashed my old one. About twenty from the school congregated in the Huitres for dinner. I sat in a corner with Guards, Chelsea Bill, and Rose, and had quite an amusing time.

Sunday, 22nd April.

Very dull church parade in the morning. After lunch I had some more music with Bonvalot and Stevenson, this time adding the Franck sonata, which I had bought in Amiens.

Monday, 23rd April.

Parade in the morning. After lunch most of the batteries went away, except the IVth Corps. I went in on one of the lorries with Menny, the Cheshire. The driver insisted on stopping every now and then, and taking pot shots at hares he could see in the fields with his rifle. He did not hit any. We had a bath (excellent), tea and dinner at the Hotel du Rhin, which was almost as good as the Godbert. Among my purchases was a book of the English Suites of Bach.

Tuesday, 24th April.

A lovely day. Sat about and played the mess piano.

Wednesday, 25th April.

Left Vaux by lorry at 11.30 after a delightful two days. We stopped for an hour in Amiens and had lunch, and then went on to Nesle. There I picked up another lorry and found the battery in a cellar in Germaine. Field was in bed, not very well. The others hale and hearty. My new watch came, and a parcel of chocolate.

Thursday, 26th April—Friday, 27th April.

A few parades. Field and I walked about a little in the evenings. We had bridge after dinner.

Saturday, 28th April.

Field went off to hospital about his eyes. Thacker and I on parade. I went round to the 8th Worcesters' headquarters for tea.

Sunday, 29th April.

Having lost the toss, I went on church parade. Then the battery, including myself, was inoculated for or against, whichever it is, typhoid. This is my second go, the last time being at Maldon. I went early to bed.

Monday, 30th April.

Woke up feeling beastly. Field walked in at breakfast, having spent his time in Amiens. In the afternoon I got up and walked over to Division for some money. We had a rather merry evening, at which I looked on from my bed. We all sleep in the mess.

Tuesday, 1st May.

Lovely day and quite hot sun. We have now had ten days without rain. The battery spent the morning cleaning itself, and after lunch

went on parade for inspection by the G.O.C., Maj.-Gen. Mackenzie. We stood behind the 4th Gloucesters. A lot of men were given pieces of paper with their valorous deeds written on them. It was quite hot standing about, but we got home by tea time.

Wednesday, 2nd May.

We played bridge in the afternoon and had an early tea preparatory to going up the line. While we were waiting to start I took the pith out of a rather trashy novel of Field's, reading some of the gems aloud, to the others' amusement. Field stayed back at Germaine. The rest of us started at 5 p.m., reaching Holnon at 9.30 p.m. I went on to a small dugout in the " Brown line," so called because it is dug out of white chalk, about a mile north of the village. We are 2,500 yards from the nearest Hun, and apparently lead a charmingly rural existence. I settled in by midnight and slept on the floor with Weeks, curled up, as space does not admit of straightening one's legs.

Thursday, 3rd May.

A lovely hot day. Thacker came up in the morning and I walked over with him to the right hand gun position, near the three cottages on the top of the ridge. I had a fine view of St. Quentin and the cathedral standing up well, in the middle, not much over 5,000 yards away. During the day Weeks and I laboured at enlarging the dugout, picking down the chalk from the far end and carting it up four stairs in sandbags—no light task. In the evening Cpl. Walters came up with a team for the right hand gun, and Thacker with them. He came into my dugout, and Wardrop and Smith from the machine gunners as well, who live close by. We drank a bottle of port I had up with me.

Friday, 4th May.

I woke very late, about 10 a.m. Thacker came up again and we went over to the right hand gun. I had another look at St. Quentin. The rest of the day was spent in digging in the dugout, and by the end we had gone back nearly three feet. We had forgotten about supporting the roof until, after tea, a large quantity of chalk fell down. Both of us were luckily clear of it when it fell, but we had a good deal of trouble carting it all away, and then propped up the ceiling with boards. I heard to-day that Clarke of the 6th Gloucesters " Tramways," was killed while on patrol in front here. I am very sorry indeed. His servant, who used to help in our mess, was killed with him.

Saturday, 5th May.

Up at 5.30 a.m. Lovely hot day again. I am in luck's way with the weather up here. Thacker and Vacher came up about 10 a.m. bringing a note from Field, who is lunching with them. During the morning I made a bed for the dugout, which is much better than sleeping on the floor. We had some excitement in the afternoon, seeing a Hun plane brought down by our Archies inside our own lines and not so very far away. I have only seen that done once before, at Laventie, " in the old days," as everyone says when speaking of that time.

Sunday, 6th May.
At 12.30 a.m. all the guns round opened up to support a raid. There is an 18-pounder battery some three hundred yards behind us, which fires almost straight over our heads with a perfectly deafening noise. They kept it up for about an hour, but nothing came back. We all stood outside to watch, since sleep was impossible. We also had a sprinkling of rain. However it was a nice clear morning. I met Thacker at 10 a.m. by the Chateau and went with him to reconnoitre a position to shoot on the Bois des Roses. To do this we had to go down a gentle slope of half a mile in which we got a perfect view of St. Quentin. We finally chose a position in the bank of a small sunken road, covered with violets, anemones and cowslips, which with the leaves of the hazels coming out, made a beautiful picture.

Monday, 7th May.
Not very well and lay on my bed most of the day. I took up a working party to dig the emplacement for the Bois des Roses. We were on from 10 p.m. to midnight. Nothing came our way except the rain, which wetted us through fairly successfully.

Tuesday, 8th May.
Rain again. Rather a headache, so I stayed indoors and read a little. At 9.45 p.m. I went out with Thacker to the 7th Worcesters battalion headquarters near Fayet to reconnoitre a position to shoot on Cepy farm. However, Dorman, the C.O., told us to come again next day, as you couldn't see much in the dark. For that matter you can't show your face above ground during the daylight.

Wednesday, 9th May.
With Thacker at 10 a.m. to Dorman's headquarters. No rain to-day. From here a guide took us through Fayet and down the St. Quentin road to one of the front line posts. Here we saw 'Tommy' of the machine gunners, looking very dirty and unshaven. They do live a dog's life up in these posts; and not too much cover either. We saw Clarke's grave here. Thacker and I then crawled up to the ridge and tried to see Cepy farm. The field in which we were was covered in little heaps of bean stalks, and there were a few dead about, some lying behind these heaps for cover from view. I took bearings on various points, including the Cathedral. We got back for lunch, going straight through Fayet and on to the monument, not all round by Battalion headquarters.
At 9.0 p.m. I took Cpl. Parsons and four other men to the position we had chosen, and dug there from 10-1, making a hole $8' \times 5' \times 5'$ deep. There was a good deal of sniping going on, but not much shelling, except away on the left, where I think they must have done a raid, to judge by the noise.

Thursday, 10th May.
Quiet day, though hot. I went down to headquarters for lunch and a bath. I believe I am more comfortable in the Brown line than they are in Holnon. Field came up for lunch, and to stay up in Vacher's place,

who is gone on leave. Field walked up with me and stayed for some tea. The 18-pounders near us co-operated in an artillery strafe from 3.0-3.15. To prevent accidents the R.F.C. went across and put down all the Hun balloons opposite, except one, as it turned out. We had a quiet night.

Friday, 11th May.
About 9.0 a.m. the Hun sent over two 4.2's, a 'short' and 'over' for the 18-pounder battery. Then at 10 he began in earnest and strafed them nearly all day, knocking out one gun, observing from his balloon. I went back to Holnon for lunch and Field came up with me afterwards and took over. I stayed for tea with him, and then went back to Holnon to sleep.

Saturday, 12th May.
Very hot. I went up to Field in the morning for a short time to get something I had left behind. At 8.30 p.m. I started out with Thacker to the line. We picked up Cpl. Parsons and his team at the Chateau cutting, and went on to the company headquarters in front of Fayet. There we found the guns, and I led off with an ammunition carrying party for a shoot on Cepy farm. Thacker was shooting from the emplacement I dug a few nights ago. I went on across the main road to a trench leading nearly up to the farm, which was supposed to have Huns in it at the far end. However there was an infantry bombing post in front of us, so we were safe enough. Zero time was 1.10 a.m. We started off and fired about seventy rounds, while the artillery put down quite a barrage on and round the farm for ten minutes. Then they lifted for the infantry to go in, and we stopped. The Hun made no reply whatever; in fact he was not in the farm at all. As soon as we had finished we cleared out, that is Parsons, Bruford, and myself, I carrying the base-plate. We joined up with Thacker again at company headquarters and went back through Fayet to Field, where I had some whiskey. Thacker and I finally got into Holnon by 4 a.m. Very tired.

Sunday, 13th May.
I stayed in bed all the morning. The cellar I sleep in is dark and delightfully cool and fresh. Field came down to lunch and to stay. Thacker went off at 2 p.m. to Attily to help at brigade. Field and I went out in the evening looking for vegetables in the neighbouring gardens.

Monday, 14th May.
Very hot, and not feeling too well. Went out a little and slept during the afternoon in the cellar. We marched back to Germaine at 9 p.m., where we found rather a mix up of billets; however we settled in by 2 a.m. Thacker remains at brigade, Vacher is on leave, Field and I are in a room together for sleep and food.

Tuesday, 15th May.
In the morning Field and I went round to 'rear brigade' to see Mortimer, the transport officer. Edge, of the 8th Worcesters, came in, and an R.E., and there was a certain amount of chaff. F. and I had a rather jolly evening, eventually going round and exhibiting ourselves at brigade in pyjamas about 9.30 p.m.

1917

Wednesday, 16th May.
Rain all day. Out a little in the evening, and early to bed.

Thursday, 17th May.
We left at 6 a.m. and marched to Nesle. F. and I again in one small room with one bed, which he has, having won the toss. We lunched at a small restaurant, quite respectably. This is the only place in the neighbourhood which the Hun did not destroy when he retired : and he crowded all the inhabitants of the country round in here. We went back to the billet and slept, both on the bed, from 2.30 to 6.0 p.m., and then emerged for dinner at the same place. After that we went round to the station, as F. wanted to see the lie of the land for to-morrow, as he is entraining officer for the brigade. Then we came in to bed.

Friday, 18th May.
Field up and off at 5 a.m. I moved into the bed then, and stayed there till 8 a.m. Then, with the battery alone, I moved off at 10 a.m. and joined up with the brigade transport column and marched some ten miles to Rouvroy. It was not too hot and we did not go too fast, and so came along fairly comfortably. We were billeted in old French gun positions, with quite good dugouts, Rouvroy being in a similar position to Herleville before the push in July, 1916. We are the only people marching, and I can't quite see why they make us do it.

Saturday, 19th May.
We started again at the reasonable hour of 10 a.m.—I fancy Mortimer has a good deal to do with the arrangement of this show—and marched to Domart sur la Luce, a long straggling village of no interest. I had sent Parsons on ahead to find our billets, and he told me on arrival that there were no officers' billets. This was about 3 p.m. I wandered up the street and at the fourth attempt found a good place, with a bed and sheets. In fact there were two beds, so I went out and found the machine gunners' transport officer—a new one, not ' the Boss '—and invited him in to share the other bed. We dined together, eggs provided by the old woman, with bread and butter, salmon and pineapple in tins, and a bottle of ' Graves ' from the village shop, finishing with half a bottle of port I had with me.

Sunday, 20th May.
Started at 8.30 a.m. on a very tiring march of seventeen miles. We halted from 11.30 to 1.0 just outside Amiens, into which we were not allowed to go. Then we went on through Amiens to Villers Bocage on the Doullens road, where I joined up with Field and Thacker again, and Butler, who has come back to us. Bed at 10, and very pleased to be there.

Monday, 21st May.
We marched off again at 8.30 a.m. to Beauval, getting in at midday. This makes sixty miles in five days on our ' flat feet,' as one says. However this is not such a bad spot : quite a town. Field and I are together in adjoining rooms, with sheets, of quite a nice house. The owner was

rather horrified to see our boots, but we assured him that no speck of dust should touch his carpet and he seemed reassured : really a very genial old fellow. We lunched at the Hotel National and then came back to the billet to sleep, later dining at the same place. We have to do an exhibition shoot to-morrow for Division, which fills me with rage, as both I and the men have already marched far enough without throwing in these little extras.

Tuesday, 22nd May.

Parade at 9 a.m. and a three mile march to a range. We worked continuously digging in and detonating till 4.30 p.m., when we did a shoot before Division and a large collection of officers and men, which was not an unqualified success. I was much too angry to care what happened, and after asking Thacker to go to brigade and protest, which he would not do, I went myself and talked to Bowyer, the Staff Captain. He was very nice and sympathetic, &c., &c., but of course did not, and could not, do anything about it, as I might have seen if I hadn't been so angry. Field, Butler and I dined again at the Hotel.

Wednesday, 23rd May.

I rode on ahead through Doullens to Sus-St. Leger. The battery arrived at 1.30 p.m. and I put them into their rather indifferent billets. At 4.0 p.m. Field and I rode back into Doullens. On the way my tyre burst, and just as I had borrowed a fresh bicycle from a sentry close by we heard the sound of a bomb swishing through the air followed by a big explosion ; and an English 'plane flew over. I suppose it was done by mistake. We rode on, had tea in a shop, bought some shirts and a book and dined in the Quatre Fils Gaymon. I picked up my bicycle again where I had left it, and heard that two French girls had been wounded by the bomb. We got in by 10 p.m., I on a flat tyre—no joke.

Thursday, 24th May.

Field on ahead billeting at 4.30 a.m. The battery started at 7. We marched from 9 to 1 p.m. down on to the main Doullens road and there got into some lorries which took us to Dainville, close to Arras. We had quite good billets. I am in the mess, Field with Thacker a little way off.

Friday, 25th May.

I stayed in bed fairly late as I was rather feeling the heat, and wanted a rest. After lunch I went into Arras with Field on a lorry. We went to the cinema, in the theatre, run by the VIth Corps, and had tea afterwards in the officers' tea room there. The place swarms with troops. I bought some things in the canteen, and we came away, getting back by 7 p.m.

Saturday, 26th May.

Parades most of the day on a training ground about a mile off. Vacher came off leave. Wyatt (Northamptons, attached 4th Gloucesters) came in to dine.

Sunday, 27th May.

Hot again. Parade in the morning, but not again. Field took an evening church parade.

Monday, 28th May.
We live in style now and run an orderly officer. It was my turn to-day, and I went into Arras before lunch for mess stuff. A man on VIth Corps bridging train gave me a lift in, in his sidecar. He said they had just finished two girder bridges over the railway by the station. On the opening day of the show the Hun put a shell into an ammunition dump under the then bridge and blew it sky high.

At 4 p.m. I started on a bus to VIth Corps school for a lecture. Evers, 8th Worcesters, was going too, and so we had a pleasant time together. We got there by 6.30 p.m. and found that the lecture had been cancelled at 6.15 p.m., so we came away; dining in Avesnes on the way back, and getting in at 9.30 p.m.

Tuesday, 29th May.
Up at 3 a.m. and to the old front line in front of Wailly for a practice attack, in which we did some live firing. There was some rain, and I got wet through. We got back by 11.30 a.m. and I slept till lunch. Nothing to do in the afternoon.

Wednesday, 30th May.
At 8.30 a.m. I went in a lorry again to VIth Corps School at Givenchy le Noble for a gas lecture. They gave an exhibition of smoke and gas, and also of flammenwerfer, a most unpleasant form of amusement. Lunch in Avesnes and back by 4.

Thursday, 31st May.
Spent the morning with Thacker reconnoitring routes. We went through Arras to Tilloy les Mofflaines on the Cambrai road, where our headquarters will be, and came back through Beaurains and Achicourt. We had some bridge in the evening.

Friday, 1st June.
I took the battery at 8 a.m. with the handcarts to our stores in Achicourt. On the way we heard and saw some big explosions near the Doullens road, which turned out afterwards to be 14-inch shells from a high velocity gun, though we had not heard the shell going over. It blew up one lorry and some ammunition. At 3 p.m. Field and I went into Arras and spent an hour at the cinema, and also had tea. He then went back, and I went on, in a lorry, to Tilloy, where I waited for the battery. I went over to an artillery canteen and bought some cake, some of which I ate. While I was waiting in our mess, a tarpaulin covered structure, the Hun sent over a few shells on to the road beyond, which were somewhat disturbing, and one, which scattered mud over the roof, quite considerably so. However nothing came any nearer. The battery arrived about 11 p.m. I slept above ground, but everyone else went down below.

Saturday, 2nd June.
A lovely day. We had a short parade in the morning. After lunch Vacher and I reconnoitred the way to forward brigade headquarters over a bare plain, with Monchy rising up in the distance. We had to wait

some time as they were shelling the place pretty freely with 5.9's; however we got through and back safe enough. We had a somewhat varied night. About 10 p.m. we had the usual few shells on to the road to catch the transport. Then at 11 p.m. a Hun squadron came over and dropped a few bombs about. At midnight we started a tremendous bombardment over on the left towards Lens, which lasted more or less till 4.30 a.m. I was not at all well and rather sorry for myself.

Sunday, 3rd June.
Feeling perfectly beastly. I had my bed moved down to a room at the far end of the dugout in which Field and Thacker are, and went and lay down from 11 to 3 p.m. I did not want to eat, and so stayed away from meals. In the afternoon the Hun shelled the wood to the west of this place, which we face. Very few people live there, but he smashed up a kind of open-air bath close by.

Monday, 4th June.
Very hot again. I not on parade, and so got up late. In the afternoon I went into Arras with Field and took some money off the Field Cashier: otherwise we had a series of disappointments, the cinema, teaplace, and our divisional show being shut.

Tuesday, 5th June.
Very hot indeed. Parade in the morning. I am tired of the war just now. There was an exciting air fight over us about 6.0 p.m. in which a Hun was brought down in flames, hit by a tracer bullet, and an English plane badly damaged. The man got down almost to the ground and then hit a wire which overturned him and broke his neck. Again a very heavy bombardment on the left at 8 p.m.

Wednesday, 6th June, to Saturday, 9th June.
Still hot. Parades each day and bombardments in the evening. Thursday Field and Thacker went off for the day to 3rd Army T.M. School, bringing back in the evening some mess stores and a case of soda water.

Saturday evening Field and I walked over to the Railway Triangle and up a valley, where we came upon a large collection of howitzers— 6-inch and 9.2-inch. We saw a number of shells with the new instantaneous fuze. A gunner was explaining them to us and kept tapping the top of the fuze with a hammer he had in his hand, which seemed rather rash, as they are supposed to be very sensitive.

Sunday, 10th June.
Nothing much to do all day. At 10 p.m. we left for Simencourt. Just as we had come out on to the road, ready to start, the Hun put over two shells, one of which seemed to land plump in our mess. Afterwards he sent over a couple more into the road on which we were standing: not too pleasant. Towards the end of our journey, at about 2 a.m., we ran into a heavy rain storm. Field met us, having been ahead to settle the billets, and conducted us in. I am in the mess with him: Thacker and Vacher together a little way down the road.

Monday, 11th June.
An easy morning. We all four went out after lunch to look for a training ground. Thacker began being childish and sulky so we left him and went off by our three selves. It was altogether very absurd. He had Field in in the evening, strafed him heartily, and said he would talk to the General about it.

Tuesday, 12th June.
Parade 7-10 a.m. Then we all came into the mess and sat in solemn conclave. We all told each other home truths and all suggested the simplest thing would be for him to give us the sack and get a new lot. Thacker behaved surprisingly sensibly, and generally we cleared the air. After lunch I walked over to Division at Warlus and tried to get a car to go on leave. I saw Rabone and Tommy Coates, but it was no good. Thacker went to brigade in the evening and came back saying we would and could arrange some working agreement. After dinner we played four-handed bridge with Butler, just come off leave.

Wednesday, 13th June.
Parade 7-10 a.m. I managed at last to get a new pair of ration boots.

Thursday, 14th June.
Said goodbye to them on parade at 9.30 a.m. and started off with Weeks for the leave train. We got a lift for the last two miles to railhead, at Agnez-les-Duisans, and I sent Weeks sadly back. After some time the train started, I in a good carriage with a Canadian captain. We stopped a good many times and were soon quite full. We reached Boulogne at 5 p.m. and just missed the boat. I went round to the Hotel Folkestone and booked a room, and then went into the town and had tea and an ice. At dinner in the hotel I sat next a rather nice fellow in the " King's " regiment, and we went out afterwards to look for a cinema or entertainment of some kind, but found none and came back. I had a large bath.

Friday, 16th June.
The King's man and I went round to the quay at 9.30 a.m., and the boat started at 10.10. We had a very good crossing with the sea like a millpond. Folkestone at 12. We came up by the second train, as the first was full, and had lunch on the way. After some difficulty at Victoria I got a taxi and drove to the Langham, starting my ten days' leave.

III

Monday, 25th June.

At the Grosvenor Hotel. Got up early, met my travelling companion, Warburton, of the King's Regiment, and went with him to the train, where we had engaged seats in the Pullman. We started at 8.50 a.m. and had breakfast on board, getting down to Folkestone by 11.30 or so. We went straight to the boat and secured our seats. Ours was the first train down, so we had the pick. Two others came along soon, the last being the staff train, and we saw General Mackenzie come along the quay followed by Tommy Coates, his A.D.C., marshalling two porters each with a large barrow load of kit. We pushed off at last and reached Boulogne at 1.30 p.m. We put our kit in the consigne and lunched at the Hotel Meurice. After that we had our hairs cut, tea, and went to the cinema, which was rather amusing. I bought two extra stars in a shop and had them sewn on then and there, as I had been gazetted lieutenant two days before. We dined at the Hotel Meurice and went to a very crowded train at 10.40 p.m.

Tuesday, 26th June.

We arrived at Agnez les Duisans, one of the Arras railheads, at 5.30 a.m., and there the R.T.O. informed me that the Division had left two days ago, and gone back. I walked to the rest camp and left some kit there, but it looked uninviting so I went back to the village and asked a woman to give me some breakfast, which she did—fried eggs and bread and butter. I went by the leave train again to St. Pol, where I had lunch at the Hotel de France, and telephoned from a kind of general exchange to division to find out where the brigade was. From there I got a lorry to Frévent and stopped there, getting the town commandant's leave to stay at the Hotel d'Amiens instead of the usual rest house. It is a picturesque, unpretentious little place, and a pretty view of green fields from my bedroom window. When I was just starting dinner Morris, brigade signals, came in, having ridden over on his motor bicycle; so we fed together.

Wednesday, 27th June.

Off at 9.0 a.m. in a supply lorry to the dump half way between Fillièvres and Linzeux, from which, to my great annoyance, I had to walk, across the fields in blazing heat to Blangermont, where I found the battery all at home and very cheery. I have quite a good bedroom to myself, with Field and Vacher sharing one down the passage in the same house. We played bridge in the evening and annoyed the landlady, who wished to shut up and go to bed at 9.0 p.m.

Thursday, 28th June.
We paraded from 9-11.30, in the afternoon, and again in the evening. After dinner we played bridge, four-handed, as Morris came in. Field and I went round with him afterwards to brigade, where we found the General and all the others seated up playing bridge.

Friday, 29th June.
All the battery on fatigue, helping the French to get in the hay. We played bridge morning and afternoon. After tea Field and I went a rather nice and gentle walk to Flers, the next village, choosing the route because we were told there were no soldiers there. In fact we did only see one. Morris came in to dinner and played bridge.

Saturday, 30th June.
Rain all day. Vacher went off on a course to 3rd Army T.M. School. We moved our mess down the road a little way into a charming house with a garden full of peas and strawberries. The old woman where we were was getting too tiresome. Life is very pleasant indeed here. We have cream and fresh fruit every day, and generally strawberries.

Sunday, 1st July.
I on church parade, and marched the battery to Linzeux to find the parade cancelled, as the battalion (8th Worcs.) was gone on a medal hunting expedition. After lunch I went on a bicycle with Thacker to St. Pol, where we had tea and dinner. We met Vacher and Butler there, having tea with them—including some splendid raspberries.

Monday, 2nd July.
I went strolling about the fields this morning with Thacker doing what is called a ' tactical exercise without troops,' a much less fatiguing operation than with them. Field and I spent the evening with some amusement concocting an article for the Daily Mail on Stokes guns.

Tuesday, 3rd July—Friday, 6th July.
Parades in the morning and usually slept in the afternoon. One day we did " O'Grady Drill," when the men are induced to think by being required to move only when the command is preceded by the words " O'Grady says."

Saturday, 7th July.
Hot again. At 2 p.m. Field and I started off on bicycles for Hesdin, which we reached at 4 p.m. The whole place was decked out with flags and we were told that the Queen had been there in the morning, looking at some hospitals. We had tea in a café and then played French billiards, with no pockets to the table. I had my hair cut and was shaved by a woman, who did it rather well. Then Field and I met again and dined at the Hotel de Commerce. During the meal the Queen passed in a car carrying a white flag, one of a long procession of Rolls-Royces. We got back by 11 p.m., helped on our way by some whisky in the A.S.C.'s billet in Fillièvres.

Sunday, 8th July.

I had nothing to do all day. The others went off on horses to St. Pol after lunch, returning about 9 p.m.

Monday, 9th July.

We all went with the battery to the 8th Worcesters to work for a week as infantry. We found it rather amusing and flattered ourselves we could do some of their tricks better than they could. I stayed and had a nice lunch with Evers and B company.

Tuesday, 10th July.

Up at 5.30 and paraded at 6.30 a.m. to join the battalion in a day's wood fighting. This was said to be quite successful, and I take it on trust, but found it rather fatiguing. We returned by 1.30 p.m., and I lunched at battalion headquarters where was the Colonel (Bilton), A. V. Rowe, now Adjutant, and Edge. I slept all the afternoon and did no more that day.

Wednesday, 11th July—Sunday, 15th July.

Thursday's chief interest was dinner, to which we had invited the Brigadier and Brigade Major, A. H. Spooner and Parry-Jones. We had quite a nice dinner for them and they made themselves very pleasant. The General told me that E. S. Rabone, late 8th Worcesters, and then on Division, has been made G.S.O. 3 of the 56th Division, which is a jolly good job for him.

Friday was a very long and extremely uninteresting brigade field day. I had to sit out all the morning in the eye of the sun, which I did not care for. Stanley, the A.S.C. Captain, and Morris, Brigade Signals, came to dine and play bridge.

Saturday we had a thunderstorm. Sunday I went to church twice. The others went to St. Pol after lunch.

Monday, 16th July.

The battery on a bombing course under Mullet, a rather quaint person with whom I spent a week near Tulloch corner in January. He has a somewhat truculent sergeant instructor, who needs 'telling off' badly. Bowyer, the Staff Captain, came to dine, and the atmosphere was, perhaps naturally, rather more free than with the General.

Tuesday, 17th July.

Very hot day. I not on parade. Weeks went away on leave, and to be married.

Wednesday, 18th July.

A holiday for the divisional races. We three started off at about 11.30 in the brigade waggonette, borrowed from their farm, with six horses, driven by Bowyer, complete with cigar. The day was rather squally, with a good many heavy showers at intervals. Most of the units had a coach of some kind, generally a G.S. waggon with painted canvas sides. The 8th Worcesters had a most realistic girl in one of their officers. Everyone was there from the G.O.C. downwards to a Punch nd Judy show, and altogether it was great fun. Betting was worked by a total-

isator by means of which I was twenty francs down at the end of the day. On the way back Parry-Jones and Bowyer, dressed as highwaymen, held up the 8th Worcesters coach with revolvers.

Thursday, 19th July—Friday, 20th July.
Both days we did some dud firing which was rather good fun, especially the second day, when we had a kind of scheme. Friday afternoon Field and I went into St. Pol on a horse and a bicycle respectively. We exchanged mounts for part of the way going in, and I did not fall off. We had our hairs cut and dined at the Hotel de France. Getting back we found Sadler, from the 7th Worcesters, who has come temporarily to take Vacher's place, Vacher having ' gone sick ' from his course.

Saturday, 21st July.
I went to Doullens for some shell jackets from our spare kit ; on a postal lorry to Frévent and than by train on. Talking of the post, while at Blangermont I have fairly often been getting the Times on the day of issue, which is a marvellous feat of organisation, I think. Letters generally take three days, occasionally two. I had tea in Doullens, a poor tea, and put up at the hotel ' Quatre Fils Gaymon.' There were some rather convivial R.F.C. people there, who lent a good deal of life to the meal.

Sunday, 22nd July.
I had an early and somewhat hurried breakfast, and then caught the 9.10 a.m. to Frévent. Here I caught the postal lorry that had brought me down, and was carried to brigade, not walking a step all the way. I found a parcel of sparklets &c. from home, for the two syphons which we maintain nowadays. Thacker and Sadler went off to St. Pol, Field and I sat in and amused ourselves with cards.

Monday, 23rd July.
Very hot. Nothing much to do in the morning. Field and I went into St. Pol in the afternoon. I had some difficulty in getting a bicycle at first as all ours were punctured, so he rode on ahead on his horse. I managed finally to get one from brigade and found him in the tea shop near the station with Tommy of the machine gunners. I played the piano a bit when the room cleared. After that we did some shopping and Tommy left us. We were firmly determined to do ourselves well at dinner, and so among other things we had a bottle of Perriet Jouet each. We rode back and finished a rather strenuous evening in the mess with Sadler.

Tuesday, 24th July.
Did not do much to-day ; played bridge a good deal.

Wednesday, 25th July.
Rain in the morning. We spent the day packing and settling up. At 4.30 p.m. we marched to Petit Houvin, entraining at 9.49 p.m. We were all together in a carriage, and had also Leck, Perry, and two other machine gunners. We played a little bridge. I was not particularly well.

ZEGGERS CAPPEL

Thursday, 26th July.

Two a.m. we arrived at Zeggers Cappel, about twenty miles west of Ypres. Here we detrained and marched about a mile to our billets. I was very angry with Field over some trifle which I forget. We settled into billets at 5 a.m. The landlady was somewhat peevish at being turned out so early, which was not surprising. I got up at 10 a.m. and stayed up till 2 p.m., when I went to bed again, feeling very nasty. Evers came in to see me about tea time and Field later on.

Friday, 27th July.

We had an inspection parade in the morning, and I slept after lunch. At tea Field pulled my leg rather hard which I did not like, so I suppose I am a trifle ill.

Saturday, 28th July.

I went out with Thacker looking for a training ground, and after lunch went back to make a sketch map of the place by compass bearings. I went a walk with Field in the evening.

A section list of this period is as follows :—

No. 5 Gun.	No. 6 Gun.
Cpl. Parsons	Cpl. Bowater
Pte. Pearce	Pte. Hughes
Miles	Wilkins (hit Wieltje, Aug. 17.)
Scadding	Short, G.
Bruford	Brotherton (cook)
	Thompson
No. 7 Gun.	No. 8 Gun.
Cpl. Guest	L.-Cpl. Walters
Pte. Hingley	Pte. Marsh
Archer	Taylor
Saunders	Britton
Saunders	
Weare	

In addition were Sgt. Williams and Pte. Weeks.

Sunday, 29th July—Monday, 30th July.

My servant, Weeks, came off leave to-day, having been married in the interval. We had rain both days, fairly heavy, and paraded in a barn near the men's billet, reading to them such things as divisional standing orders, gas orders, &c. After dinner I smoked a cigar, which I did not like much.

Tuesday, 31st July.

Off at 8.30 a.m. to a practice attack by the 4th Gloucesters. Field went on leave. My show was rather a farce, and I did not do much. Capt. Foweraker gave me lunch, a very good one, after marching back with his company, which has its own little band of three or four penny whistles. They make a quaint and rather plaintive sound, and not in the least martial. I sent my men home under Sgt. Williams, and after lunch walked over with Dudle, a Manchester, one of Foweraker's subalterns, to the ground for the coming brigade practice attack, and made some arrangements with the Gloucesters about it. I got back by 5.30 p.m.

Wednesday, 1st August.

We all got up in pouring rain at 6.30 a.m. for this brigade attack. I had only got a quarter of a mile down the road when I met someone who told me it was cancelled, for which many thanks. The rain continued all day. Thacker introduced a new game called Hoggenheimer, a violent gamble, at which I succeeded in winning sixty francs. We had the first telegrams through about the Ypres show, which began yesterday.

Thursday, Friday, Saturday, 2nd, 3rd and 4th August.

Wet each day. Saturday Thacker rode off on a push bike to see his uncle, who commands XIXth Corps Artillery. Evers came in to dine and we had a delightful evening. Thacker arrived in the middle of dinner, having come most of the way in his uncle's car. He was taken up to Ypres and other interesting places and saw quite a lot.

Sunday, 5th August.

No rain to-day for a wonder. The Ypres show appears to have been brought more or less to a standstill by the mud. I had a long conversation with the landlady to-day, who is not so hostile as she was. She commented on the number of Englishmen to be seen about in this country and said : " N'est-ce pas que l'Angleterre est vide ?" which I thought a wonderful idea. I said I thought there were one or two people left there. She seemed surprised that I knew to-day was Sunday, though I had not been to Messe. She had seen one of our military services and described it as drôle. She said it was too odd to see everyone sitting or lying on the ground, and then suddenly they were " tous debout et chantants."

Monday, 6th August.

The brigade practice attack came off at last. We had to get up at an absurd hour to be in position by 8 a.m. It was rather better run than usual, even low-flying aeroplanes, flares, &c. We succeeded in trampling down a lot of corn, which not unnaturally annoyed the local inhabitants who hoped to live on it. We had a long and rather strange speech from Hunter-Weston, the corps commander, who made us all repeat after him in chorus the phrase : " The natural corollary of delegation of authority is intelligent supervision."

Tuesday, 7th August.

Was a blind day, with nothing done or to do.

Wednesday, 8th August.

After tea I went over to Rubrouck for a lecture. I started on a bicycle, which soon showed itself to be punctured, and so I left it at a battalion headquarters and walking on a little way was picked up by an ambulance. The lecture, a most interesting one, was given by Brig. Gen. Stockwell, on the Ypres show, opening day, when his brigade went through another in the Wieltje sector and took the line Winnepeg-Kansas Cross, but were driven back again. Gen. Mackenzie was there and, speaking afterwards, hinted that we might become more closely acquainted with the locality later on. I walked back a little way, and luckily got another lift in an ambulance, thus saving a wetting in an exceptionally heavy thundershower.

Thursday, 9th August—Sunday, 12th August.

Nothing very much to do. Sunday Bradford of the 4th Gloucesters came in to dinner.

Monday, 13th August.

A two-hour route march in the morning, in which we wandered into the French area and saw numbers of strange looking French soldiers. We came back at 11.30 a.m. to find Field back off leave. Wardrop, M.G.C., dined and bridged.

Tuesday, 14th August.

Nice day. Made preparations to move. Mortimer and Stallard, transport officers of brigade and 8th Worcesters respectively, came in to lunch. After tea I went over to the 8th Worcesters' headquarters to get an identity disc, and had some chaff with Major Davies and the Colonel. When I got back Capt. Walford, 8th Worcesters, walked in about 7 p.m. and seemed inclined to stay the night. Stallard also came in again, and the Old Gent started off on a long series of stories about different Worcestershire people he knew, but as no one else knew them, or cared, he became rather tedious. It was raining slightly: however by repeatedly pressing on him offers of Burberry's, ground sheets, &c., &c., and giving explicit directions of the way to Evers' billet we managed to get him off by about 8 o'clock.

Wednesday, 15th August.

We left Zeggers Cappel at 5.45 a.m., entraining not far off at 7 a.m. We only just managed to squeeze on to the train. Thacker was elsewhere and Vacher gone on ahead. Field and I settled down on the untarred portions of the floor of a cattle truck amid a crowd of 8th Worcesters, and reached Poperinghe at 11 a.m. There Vacher met us, and saying it was only a kilometre to the camp, led us round about four to some tents in a field on the other side of the town. One of the features of the camp is a hole made by a 14-inch dud. We share the camp with the machine gunners. Field and I went into the town and lunched at Skindles, afterwards going back to the camp and playing four-handed bridge with Leck, who commands the machine gunners now. Thacker turned up about tea time, and he, Vacher and I went to dine at La Poupée in the Square. Leck came in and made a fifth at a very jolly dinner. I shared a tent with Field.

Thursday, 16th August.

I went ahead up the Ypres road on a bicycle, starting about 9.0 a.m. to Goldfish Chateau, some two miles short of Ypres. Kippon, the M.G., came with me. The road was crammed all the way with a double stream of traffic, lorries, ammunition waggons, men marching and riding—an extraordinary sight. We were given a small part of the garden to live in. The battery arrived about 12.30 p.m. and we pitched a tent for the officers, and some trench shelters or " bivvies " for the men. Brigade are in the Chateau. We had had our first shells in the morning before starting, some 6-inch H.V. coming over into the field next to our tents. They seemed to be mostly duds, but shook the ground even at two hundred

yards. Then after going to bed about 10 p.m. we had some more over us, which seemed to be grazing the top of the tent pole, though really going on to a dump a quarter of a mile back. Field and I each bought a pocket chess board in Pop. with little flat men made of celluloid which slip into pockets on the board. We each have our board and say what our moves are. The chief feature of the place seems to be the aeroplanes : we saw twenty-five up together this afternoon.

Friday, 17th August.
To-day we went up to the line. I went on ahead with Parsons and Bache after tea, Field and Vacher coming as far as the far side of Ypres with me. Field is staying back, near Vlamertinghe. I got a lorry most of the way. Near St. Jean there is a battery of 6-inch guns firing across the road, and they say transport drivers are recommended to bend their heads when passing, to avoid being hit. I arrived at last at Wieltje, an enormous dugout with long passages, all electrically lit, and an engine for pumping out the water which trickles in. The place, though huge, is very crowded, and I had considerable difficulty in finding any room for ourselves or the battery. They arrived at 12.15 a.m., rather disturbed, having had a shell in among the men causing five casualties. We managed to unload the limbers and get in without further mishap.

Saturday, 18th August.
In the morning Thacker and I went out first to the 4th Glos. battalion headquarters in Call Reserve, the old German support line, and then up to Capricorn trench, his main second position, where we saw some of the 4th Glos., including Capt. Foweraker. The whole place is inconceivably battered about, in spite of vast quantities of concrete : many dead to be seen, and everything soaked through with the recent rains and horrible. We came back up the Gravenstafel road and across country to Uhlan farm, where Col. Bilton lives in a ghastly little concrete hole facing the wrong way, of course, and half full of stinking water. Near there, on the way back, we saw three tanks close together, put out of action. We got inside one of them—a 'female' with Lewis guns. After lunch I went out to our old front line, just in front of this dugout, and stood with the F.O.O. of a 6-inch howitzer battery engaged in shelling Wurst farm. We could see it all very well through glasses. A telephonist at his elbow would say, "Number one fired, sir," and then count the time for the shell's flight to himself and say 'gone,' or some such word, and we saw a cloud of dust close to the farm, really a concrete dugout. The officer gave his correction, which was repeated down the 'phone, and then another shell went over. At one moment the Hun turned a barrage on to one of our forward trenches and things began to liven up. All our guns, far and near, chimed in, and the whole of the opposing ridge became a mass of smoke with our retaliation. I stayed till the Bosch put some heavy shrapnel over our trench, and then went in to tea ! After tea I went over with Vacher to Uhlan farm to see about some shoot he wanted. On our way back we stopped at a Bosch M.G. emplacement and took a look at the country. We were spotted, I suppose, because they put over a couple of shells from a 5.9 gun. We jumped down into a dugout near by already

half smashed in, and waited with some 8th Worcs. who were there. About a dozen more shells came along, all quite close. We waited a minute or two and then ran for it, and were greeted with two or three more. I ran like a hare, and when very much blown pulled up close to Evers, who was sitting in a shell hole with some of his company close by. We had a good laugh together, and then I joined up with Vacher who had fled in a different direction, and we went back to the dugout. At 8.30 p.m. Vacher left for his shoot. I went on top and watched for some time, and saw the planet Venus very well nearly due west. There was a good deal of shelling on our part, but not much coming back.

Sunday, 19th August.

Early this morning the divisions right and left pushed on a bit. Thacker and I went down to Call farm again, and the Hun put over a lot of shrapnel for our especial benefit. We also heard that the 4th Glos. B company show at Pond farm was a failure, Duddle the Manchester being killed. There is a heavy M.G. post behind it. Not out again till 8.30 p.m., when I started with a carrying party of about twenty men to Wine House. We went down the Gravenstafel road and along Capricorn trench. Just as the whole party had got into the trench the Hun put down a barrage on either side of us—on the Steenbecque, a miserable little muddy ditch about three hundred yards to our left, and on Capricorn support trench, some hundred and fifty yards to our right. We scrambled along without any casualty until the trench became nearly thigh deep in water, and shockingly battered about. We got out then and went along on our side of the trench, below the parapet, until we came to Wine House, where we dumped the shells. To come back we followed a tape—a common way of indicating a path hereabouts—leading back at right angles to Capricorn trench. This finally landed us on a road in the next division's area. I had not the slightest idea where we were, but after some enquiry and rather anxious waiting managed to get back down Admiral's road and so in, without a casualty. I don't care much about these night journeys.

Monday, 20th August.

Miller, O.C. 184th Battery, came up in the morning. Vacher got away in the afternoon with the handcarts. Thacker and I started at 8.30 p.m. with the rest, about eight men. We began badly, as the Hun started to shell the dugout entrances just as we were coming up. Fortunately I knew of another way, so we descended again and went along a very long passage, past an underground dressing station, and came out about three hundred yards down the St. Jean road, which was much better. Coming through St. Jean was rather anxious work. Twice they put some H.E. shrapnel over us, but did no harm, and we reached Goldfish Chateau safely by 10.30 p.m. The Hun shelled us a bit in the night, some coming fairly close and spattering mud on to the tent.

Tuesday, 21st August.

Not a good night, and not feeling too bright this morning. Field appeared about 9 a.m. and we played two games of chess. He went back for his lunch and came up again at 2, staying on till 7. Thacker and Vacher went to Poperinghe, returning about 10.30 p.m. Field and I lay

against the edge of the tent reading. Presently the Hun began to put 5.9 hows. into the garden, most of them fifty to an hundred yards away. We could hear them coming for about ten seconds, making a tremendous roar as they came down, and I found myself half involuntarily pressing back against the tent as if to get out of the way. Each one seemed as if it would land on my stomach, though the nearest was about thirty yards off. The 8th Worcs. had several casualties.

Wednesday, 22nd August.
Much the same programme as yesterday, though this time the excitement was caused by a squadron of Hun planes about two thousand feet up in broad daylight, and dropping bombs, but none very close. None of our planes were about and the Archies silent. The Huns wheeled slowly round and went home again. The 184th Brigade attacked in the early morning without materially altering the situation.

Thursday, 23rd August.
Breakfast in bed. Field came up again in the morning, and we played some more chess. Thacker went on ahead to Wieltje at 2.30 p.m., and Vacher and I brought up the battery an hour later, getting up by 5 p.m. without any difficulty. Vacher and I tossed up for the line and he lost. I had to go up to do a shoot in Pommern redoubt. I started at 8.30 p.m. and went to Bank farm. There the men stayed in shelter, and I went on with Pte. Bruford to Bn. Hq. in Pommern and waited for Col. Dorman till 12. He then told me there was nothing to do, so we came away. Nothing came over near us though we were shelling pretty freely. The 7th Worcs. were relieving the Bucks and there were swarms of men about, so it was extremely lucky the Hun was quiet. We got back by 1 a.m., very hot and tired.

Friday, 24th August.
Not out in the morning. Had a good wash. Thacker went up to see Vacher, who is somewhere in front of Capricorn Keep and does not enjoy it. At 8.45 p.m. I met eight mules on top and after loading up took them down Oxford road to the mule track leading to Pommern. This apparently came to an end in about an hundred yards. After some search and anxiety I found a road further down which took us as far as the old German support line. Here these beastly animals were defeated by a little loose wire and a trench, and so we had to unload and I sent them back. After wandering across country for some time we found a track marked by white posts leading towards the line. I had seventeen men with me and so was rather anxious about the Hun, especially crossing the Steenbecque, his principal barrage line. We met a stray Scot who gave us an idea of the direction—we had been swerving out to the right too much—and we began to go uphill, past some concrete dugouts. I wondered whether we should walk into a Hun post, but presently, to my great relief, we came upon Dorman's headquarters, where I was last night. From there I was given a guide to A Coy.'s headquarters—a large shell hole—and from there on to Somme farm, passing through the remains of an orchard, walking on the top all the time. Here I found a trench full of 7th Worcs. and an officer, 2/Lt. Stone. I found it extremely hard to reckon my

position; however I determined to go to a dud tank near by, which had a trench running directly back from it. I went back and fetched the men over, and dumped all the shells. Just as we had done this, and were ready to go back, suddenly we saw bombs bursting, apparently just in front of the infantry's trench. It appeared as though the Hun were coming across, though it turned out afterwards that they were some way farther off at Aisne House, which the Worcesters were trying to rush. Some of my men declared they saw the Huns advancing and one or two were rather perturbed: however that soon passed. The Hun, meanwhile, sent up his S.O.S., a rocket bursting into two red stars, and almost immediately opened up a good stiff barrage, all of which was behind us, though one or two shells were short enough to bespatter us with earth. We replied with our S.O.S., and then for three-quarters of an hour there was a fine row. I put all my men in the trench, lying flat, as it was not very deep, and hoped for the best, which was granted us. Towards the end the Hun sent up golden rain rockets, and his barrage died down, so that soon after midnight things were fairly quiet. The 18-pounders of our own barrage had been dropping very short occasionally, so we were glad to move across into the infantry trench. From there, about 12.30 a.m., I sent on Parsons with eight men and followed with the rest about five minutes later. At the infantry company headquarters we picked up two R.E.'s who knew the way back through Bank farm, and set off. We wasted little time on the way, and caught up Parsons by Uhlan farm. Nothing more came our way and we finally arrived at the dugout at 1.30 a.m., more thankful than I can say, with no casualties.

Saturday, 25th August.
After lunch I went with Thacker to the headquarters of the 8th Worcs. and 4th Glos., both in reserve now. A fine hot day. At 6.30 p.m. I went to Bank House, Dorman's headquarters, with Parsons and Bowater and their teams, Scadding, Bruford, Weare, and Hughes, Taylor, Saunders. I stayed in a dugout near Dorman's headquarters till 9.30 p.m., and then, having sent Bowater back, started up to Somme farm again. Here we left the gun in a shell hole behind a concrete wall a yard thick and went across to fetch the ammunition from the place we had left it in yesterday. We carried back thirty-six rounds and laid the gun more or less in shelter of the wall. The show, another attempt to get Aisne and one or two more small concrete places, began at 11 p.m. with a tremendous, awe-inspiring bombardment, including M.G.'s firing tracer bullets (by accident, I should think), such as I had never heard before. It was a very magnificent sound and sight. The Hun sent up a quantity of S.O.S. signals and opened up in earnest with a 5.9 barrage on the line of Dorman's headquarters or thereabouts. Nothing came our way at all, except an occasional gust of M.G. fire. The infantry went over to Gallipoli, Aisne, and Schuler galleries, and failed in every case. The Scots, on our right, charged Gallipoli, cheering twice, but could not get in: a very wonderful but terrible thing to have heard. We stayed up there till 4 a.m. and then came away in peace.

Sunday, 26th August.

Slept from 5 a.m. till midday with a break for breakfast. After lunch I went round to see Roy Holcroft, on brigade in another part of this dugout, whom I found very cheery and amusing. The post came up at tea time and a note from Field, who has kept me supplied daily. At 8.30 p.m. I left Wieltje with my two teams, Parsons' and Bowater's—the same men as two days ago—in the rain, which began almost at that moment. I was not wearing my trench coat, and so by the time we had crossed the old British front line was nearly wet through. We tailed on behind D company of the 8th Worcs., and took two and a half hours to reach Bank farm—distance about two thousand yards. Crossing the Steenbecque barrage line at a snail's pace with plenty of halts was not very inspiring: besides which the ground was disgustingly greasy. However, we got along without mishap, and I managed to squeeze the men into some concrete dugouts near by. I went to battalion headquarters in a two-room concrete place close by on the left of Pommern redoubt. Here I found Dorman, whose battalion was holding the line, and Bilton, whose battalion was going over, and a seething crowd of other people, all struggling about. I managed to get to speech with Bilton, who told me I wasn't wanted at all and could do what I chose.

Monday, 27th August.

Fairly early in the morning I managed to get on to a bed and lay there, not sleeping, which under the circumstances was impossible, but talking to people round. About 7.0 a.m. I had some breakfast, Edge, of the 8th Worcs., who seemed to be the calmest person there, giving me some tea, and a piece of bread with a sausage on it. I stayed on in the dugout till 12.45 p.m., when I moved up with my teams to a trench running parallel to and some fifty yards behind the rear hedge of Somme farm. Here I found a large number of Worcesters, the supporting company, in fact, whose jumping off place it was. I started talking to the man next to me and not for a minute or two did I discover he was an officer as he had on a Tommy's tunic and trousers, which the infantry officers wear nowadays in an attack. He said he had only been out a month, so I asked him if he had seen Zig Zag, the revue of the moment. He had not, and I spent some time describing it until our barrage opened, at 1.55 p.m. The infantry moved forward at once and I collected my lot together and sat down to wait, having instructions to move forward when the final position was taken. The Huns opened up in six or seven minutes—rather slow for a counter-barrage—and all their stuff went ' over,' which I had expected, and which was the reason I had moved forward from the dugout. Rain had been going on gently all the time, and the air was rather misty. We watched the Hun putting some tremendously heavy shrapnel on to the Gravenstafel road, but very little came our way. In about an hour the infantry began to come back, having failed to capture these machine gun strong posts. They were for going right back, but I stopped them at my trench and made them get in, rather expecting the Bosch to follow up. Fairly soon, to my great relief, an infantry sub. turned up and got in beside me. A fair number of wounded came through and went on behind.

The infantry sub., Tetlow, of C company 8th Worcs., seemed quite to know what to do. We sent down the trench for an S.O.S. rocket, which was passed up, in case. There was one available Lewis gun, but no Vickers, and some infantry in Somme trench, where I had been two nights before, further forward. At 5 p.m. our guns opened up again with a tremendous barrage and the Hun replied, this time with his barrage a little shorter than before : at least we had a good many more shells close up to us than before. Presently Cyril Holcroft came in from in front hit in the chest by a grazing bullet, and stayed some time. He went back about 7.0 p.m. to get dressed. By now the rain had increased a good deal, and the trench we were in, entirely unrevetted, was quite awful. Some four feet deep to begin with, it was now about two feet deep in semi-liquid mud. In this we sat, wet through and bitterly cold. The infantry had rather got their tails down. I had sent one message off to Thacker at Pond farm earlier in the afternoon, by Hughes and Weare, but they had not come back. Tetlow and I sent one or two messages back to his battalion hq., but only with difficulty, as everything, paper, matches (it was getting dark now), envelopes, &c., being sodden. Time passed till about 10 p.m., when a message came from battalion in answer to one of mine. We took about quarter of an hour trying to make a match light, and then found it said I was to stay up in the line with my men as riflemen. I sent Parsons back with his gun to ask if we could not go out as we had been in the line a good deal longer than the infantry and the men had had about as much as they could stand, as had I, for that matter. Presently the barrage died down somewhat, after being on for about five hours, though the rain continued as steadily as ever. Presently an officer of the 7th Worcs. came up, and with Tetlow moved forward to Somme trench. Then Honeysett and Guest, two of our reserve men, came up from battalion to say that we must stay in the line. I did not want to do this, if possible, and so went back myself to Dorman and explained the case to him. He considered a moment and then finally said I could remain down where I was, for which I was profoundly thankful. I was in such a state of mud and wet and beastliness that I hardly knew what I was doing. I was given some whiskey, bully beef and biscuits, and finally went to sleep on half a bed, sharing it with a gunner liaison officer.

Tuesday, 28th August.

The 8th Worcesters had something under three hundred casualties, including Evers very seriously wounded. Orders came from Thacker, brought by a runner, to go across to Pond farm and arrange with Vacher for one of us to stay on. At that moment I managed to get him on the telephone and said where I was and all about it. At 8.30 a.m. I moved over with Bowater's team plus Guest and Honeysett to Pond farm. The ground was dreadful, and I was pretty well played out by the time I got there, carrying the gun about half way. Vacher met us outside the dugouts and took me in. I decided that he should go out and I stay, as I had been out the whole time before. He seemed fairly cheery. I settled myself in the 182nd machine gunners' dugout, one of a gallery of reinforced concrete places rather like the arches under a railway viaduct—each arch being one dugout—facing the wrong way of course. Vacher

went away fairly soon : so did the O.C. machine gunners, leaving a section subaltern, Poole by name. The dugout is about two inches deep in water, and has a filled sandbag as a kind of stepping stone to the door. On one side there is a kind of triclinium or sloping shelf, which serves as bed, table, and chair. The place is pretty strong and seems to have kept out a good deal. We had some shells over at tea time, but no direct hits. I rather expected to be relieved to-night, but heard to the contrary. However I am only keeping two corporals and eight men—Sgt. Eves, Cpl. Guest, Ptes. Weeks, Guest, Honeysett, Bowen, Norwood, Allen G., Wright, and Donovan—which is better than having the whole lot up. I took off my boots and socks for an hour or two in the afternoon to dry my feet ; but my clothes are still all caked in mud.

Wednesday, 29th August.
At 3 a.m. the Hun began to shoot on these dugouts with L.H.V. and 4.2's, gradually increasing till 5 a.m., when he seemed to have a barrage down. I imagine that he thought we should attack at dawn. I felt perfectly beastly. We started a shoot ourselves about lunch time and kept it up pretty briskly till 4.15 p.m., when it died down a bit. They don't seem able to let their beastly guns alone for two minutes. Poole, the 182nd M.G., was relieved at 9 p.m. by Caswell of 184th, a very cheery soul. The infantry also relieved, and in the middle of the night two of them were thrust in upon us.

Thursday, 30th August.
Nothing to do in the morning. I was relieved at 7 p.m. by 182. I sent the men off two by two and reached Wieltje by 8.10 p.m. By the greatest good luck we caught a lorry within an hundred yards of the dugout, which took us right down to the main cross roads in Ypres. We then went to the asylum and got a train from there to Brandhoek. I travelled on the engine. Cpl. Medland met us and showed us into huts. The officers have a splendid palace with a mess at one end, and then a passage opening out into cubicles on each side, of which there are enough and to spare for all of us.

Friday, 31st August.
Got up in time for lunch. Vacher and I went into Poperinghe, did some shopping and had tea. Then the other two joined us for an excellent dinner at La Poupée. We could not get a lorry to take us back and had to content ourselves with the trail of an 8-inch howitzer, drawn by a tractor : not the smoothest method of travel one has known. I had eight eggs in my pocket, but only four survived the journey.

Saturday, 1st September.
Lazy morning. Thacker went on leave, and Field went into Poperinghe with him. Vacher and I walked down to brigade after tea ; and I saw Evers in a C.C.S. near by.

Sunday, 2nd September.
After breakfast Field and I went round to see his old battalion—the 5th Manchesters—who have come up here. In the afternoon Vacher and I went into Poperinghe and bought a new gramophone—a Dekka—quite

a good one, and some records. Field's friend, Widdowes, from the Manchesters, came to dinner and was quite amusing talking about Egypt, where his division was, and the "desert-canaries," the men's name for the camels.

Monday, 3rd September.
Parades all the morning, and for an hour after lunch ; and then played bridge. In the evening we three went round to some Archies near by. They fired at some Hun planes which came over, and there were dozens of searchlights flickering about. We stood close behind the gun as it fired. The colour of the flash is extraordinarily beautiful for a fraction of a second, and then one is blinded for about five minutes.

Tuesday, 4th September.
Very hot. On parade most of the day. We had a lecture on the Lewis gun from Sgt. Elliot of the 8th Worcs. Field dined with the Manchesters, and I went to bed fairly early.

Wednesday, 5th September.
Parades again. Field and Vacher into Poperinghe. Capt. Foweraker of the 4th Glos. came in for a short time after tea. I dined with the 8th Worcs., who live in the same field as we do. It was their third anniversary dinner. There were quite a fair number of originals there, including Stevenson from Division, and Roy Holcroft from Brigade. Rabone could not come—with the 56th Division. I sat next Major Davies and Roy Holcroft and had quite a gay time, finishing about 11 p.m.

Thursday, 6th September.
Field and Vacher returned early this morning. We had an appalling mixture of drinks last night, with the result that I was not quite so spry as usual. Parades again, with Lewis gun instruction. At dinner time we had a heavy thunderstorm, and rain all night.

Friday, 7th September.
Packed up in the morning and made ready to go. At 5.30 p.m. Weeks and I and Cpl. Chudleigh went on ahead in a lorry to Canal bank and found dugouts for ourselves. I managed to get two stretchers from a neighbouring dressing station for Field and myself as beds. Vacher is staying down. I walked to the cross roads and met Field with the battery at about 10.30 p.m. A quiet night. In writing to my mother to-day for her birthday I quoted from one of the men's letters a few days ago the rather unusual sentiment that " he hoped she had received the £1 he had sent a few days before ' in recognition of the unfailing kindness and generosity she had always shewn him.' " It never would have occurred to me to talk to her like that.

Saturday, 8th September.
Quite a fog all the morning. Some of the men bathed in the canal, which lies just outside our door. In the afternoon Field and I walked up to find out the way to Wieltje, as we expected to go up in the evening : we had had no orders either way. Field went to see Parry-Jones, the Brigade Major, who turned up at 6.30 and said we were to stay where we were, which is most satisfactory.

Sunday, 9th September.
A lovely day. We stayed on the Canal bank all day, playing a little chess and reading. Late in the day the gramophone came up, which we put outside and played to the men, who seemed to like it.

Monday, 10th September.
Field bathed in the Canal this morning. I was more modest and bathed in my own rubber bath. We played chess again, read, and generally passed the time very happily. There was a big strafe at 4 p.m. lasting till 6 p.m. We are in the region of 6-inch guns and get the full benefit of the noise. Peaceful night.

Tuesday, 11th September.
Chess again; Field generally wins. We strolled about a little after dinner, finally coming back to Col. Bilton, who lives next door. We took in the gramophone and played bridge. They have an American doctor now, with large horn-rimmed spectacles.

Wednesday, 12th September.
Colder to-day. Field went down to Goldfish at 2 p.m. and I followed at 4 p.m. after having tea with Col. Bilton, which he kindly offered me, as we were all packed up. We reached Goldfish at 5 p.m. They have made some small evil-smelling dugouts in the garden now. We had dinner, played one game of chess, and slept.

Thursday, 13th September.
Starting at 9.30 a.m. we moved back, marching to the same tents near Poperinghe in which we were on August 15th. Field and I lunched in the town and then came back to arrange things. I fixed up a billet for myself in an estaminet close by, as I hate tents, and it had begun to rain. Field and I again into Poperinghe, dining at La Poupée. Thacker turned up in the middle of the meal and joined us. Field came to my bedroom and slept on the floor.

Friday, 14th September.
An early start. Thacker and I on the brigade lorry bound for a place on the map near Hillock. The lorry missed the way and so I had to leave it and strike across country to meet the Staff Captain. I missed him and spent an hour rushing round the country looking for him. I found him at last, just in time to meet the battery. We are in tents again, in the same field as brigade—a little too close, perhaps, for complete comfort. The other three went off to Poperinghe for dinner, and I asked Morris, Brigade Signals, in. He came bringing a bottle of champagne, and we had quite a pleasant evening with the gramophone.

Saturday, 15th September—Sunday, 16th September.
On Saturday I dined at La Poupée with Field, and on Sunday went on church parade, and to the Celebration afterwards.

Monday, 17th September.
We moved to a farm north of Cassel. I went on ahead on a bicycle with Cpl. Bowater. We arrived in very good time, crossing the Belgian frontier with immense satisfaction. I had a meal prepared for them and

we dined in fine style—hors d'œuvres, salmon rissoles, chicken, stewed fruit, custard and cream, and dessert. Thacker and I sleep in a big hay barn, the other two in the house.

Tuesday, 18th September.

I started at 11 a.m. to reconnoitre the way to Bavinchove station, the other side of a spur of Cassel Hill, struggling back at 2 p.m. after a rather tiring walk. Field and I could not resist going into Cassel after tea. We walked over to the main road and caught an empty staff car which whisked us up there in quarter of an hour. We did some shopping, and on the spur of the moment went in and had our photographs taken. We dined in a fairly tolerable hotel, and during the meal Vacher came in, having been into Poperinghe for some gramophone records. We walked back part of the way, and then they got a lift on a motor bicycle and sidecar.

Wednesday, 19th September.

Breakfast at 6.30 a.m. We marched to Bavinchove station and after a long rest entrained, starting at 12.41. On the way south we passed through Berguette, my first detraining place in this country, and reached Arras at 6.30 p.m., and from there marched to the same billets in Simencourt that we inhabited in June. The owners welcomed us very kindly and gave us some most excellent cider. I slept in the mess with Field, as before.

Thursday, 20th September.

We got up late, having nothing much to do. I took a kit inspection in the afternoon and we played bridge, at which I lost a good deal.

Friday, 21st September.

Thacker and Field off in the morning to reconnoitre the line. I took an inspection parade, and then at 2 p.m. started on a bicycle for the Field Cashier at Etrun, Corps Hq. He made me go all the way back to Division in Duisans to get the form countersigned, which was most absurd nonsense and very annoying. I went on into Arras and bought some whiskey. Then I went for tea to the Officers' Club, a new one since we were here before, in a sort of public garden with an ornamental pond in it, now drained. The club seems very good, and has carpets and nice chairs, and the waiters are dressed in white, looking clean and nice.

Saturday, 22nd September.

We moved at 10.30 p.m. to St. Nicholas' camp, on the north side of Arras, getting there by 2 p.m. I share a tent with Thacker. I took three men and a handcart to the canteen for the whiskey I bought yesterday. After tea we all went in to see "The Duds," the 17th Divisional concert party, where they had five girls all dressed up who drew much applause. Thacker and I left at half-time for dinner in the Officers' Club: the others came in later on.

Sunday, 23rd September.

Hot day. I spent an hour and a half trying to get through on the 'phone to the Staff Captain about some rations. Field and Vacher went

up to the line at 1 p.m. I for once am staying back. I had tea with Thacker at the Officers' Club; and then he went up the line and I back to the camp where I dined with brigade, playing bridge afterwards and winning three francs off the General.

Monday, 24th September.
At 9 a.m. I started on a lorry with Edge of the 8th Worcs and Richards, a 183 machine gunner, to go to Doullens for the brigade surplus kit. We had lunch there and came back by 6.30. On the way back the driver insisted on going so near the edge of the road that we all expected to go into the ditch, and at last Edge took the wheel and drove a few miles. I dined with him at the Club.

Tuesday, 25th September.
The Hun put half a dozen rounds of 6-inch H.V. stuff into the camp this morning, so Edge and I thought it would be a good thing to have a bath at the Club. After lunch I went up the line and joined Thacker at rear headquarters. I had to go through a very long trench to reach him, getting a good view once or twice of the country in front. He has quite a nice comfortable little place near the bottom of one of the main communication trenches. He took me up the line after tea and we saw Field and Vacher.

Wednesday, 26th September.
Breakfast at 9 a.m. I went up the line on my own account, exploring, this morning, and joined Thacker at 1.30 p.m. after going through miles of trenches. We went up forward again together later on.

Thursday, 27th September.
At 10.30 a.m. I went up the line and took over from Field, who came down about 2 p.m. We are in a dugout with the machine gunners in the support line. There was a little retaliation fire in the afternoon, and I did some registering at 6.0 p.m. The night was quiet. I spent from 8 p.m. to 1 a.m. wandering round the guns.

Friday, 28th September—Saturday, 29th September.
Nothing much to do beyond the usual firing.

Sunday, 30th September.
At 1.0 a.m. quite suddenly the Hun opened a heavy barrage of light T.M.'s on the brigade front, on the front line and Charlie support where our dugout is. I was just going along this trench when it began and was nearly knocked over by a bit of shell which hit my tin hat and made a small hole in it. We put up our S.O.S. and there was a general noise for about an hour. I don't think he tried to come over. I went round the left sector in the morning with Vacher as he goes out to-day to go on leave and I lost the toss for it with Field.

Monday, 1st October.
Field came up at 11.30 a.m. and Vacher went away. We both shot at 5 p.m. and observed from near the company dugout in Cry trench. I did not go round at night.

ARRAS

Tuesday, 2nd October—Wednesday, 3rd October.

Tuesday I went down to Thacker for lunch and a bath. Rain began in the evening, making the line very slippery and difficult to move in.

Thursday, 4th October.

We handed over to 184th Brigade and came out by 2 p.m. Field and I fairly ran down Chili Avenue. We are in tents in a camp on the north side of the Scarpe and east of St. Nicholas : Thacker in one, he and I in the other. We all three dined at the Officers' Club.

Friday, 5th October.

Up at 8.30 a.m. to take the men to the baths. I left them there and went on to the Club and had one myself. Oddly enough I met there a Scots officer of the 15th Division who had strayed into Bilton's dugout at Ypres on the night before the show, having lost his way. I lunched with him afterwards. We three again dined at the Club, and Field and I went to the cinema, run by XVIIth Corps.

Saturday, 6th October.

I went detonating at 9 a.m. and saw a couple of very pleasant gunners on D.A.C. who live in a delightful Nissen hut fitted up almost like a house. As before we lunched and dined at the Club. We have now got a favourite waiter who looks after us almost with affection ! Field and I went to the Spades in Arras theatre, run by the 12th Division. There is an extraordinarily good girl there, a L.-Cpl. in the Middlesex I believe, who sings and dances. He, or she rather, made eyes at the officers in one of the stage boxes, took a cigarette case from the ledge, and threw the contents to some men in the front row of the pit. The whole show is very good.

Sunday, 7th October.

Field and Thacker went off early to Amiens for the day. Corps runs a train from here, which is surprisingly thoughtful of them. I went detonating as usual. It rained hard all day so I stayed in my tent until the evening, when I dined at the Club with Ossy Constable of the 8th Worcs.

Monday, 8th October.

Detonating again. Lunch with the machine gunners. Still raining. Tea and dinner at the Club.

Tuesday, 9th October.

Up at 4.30 a.m. alone and caught the 6.15 train to Amiens. We passed through most interesting country, going close to Loupart wood, where the Hun kept his heavy guns in December, 1916; then on past the ' wrong ' end of the ravine, Aveluy, &c. I lunched at the Huitres, did some shopping and wandered about, into the Cathedral. I dined rather hurriedly at the Godbert and came back by the 8 o'clock train, getting in by midnight.

Wednesday, 10th October—Thursday, 11th October.

Field to Amiens. I took his instruction class. Thacker and I dined at the Club, sitting at a table with two rather pleasant Canadians down from St. Eloi.

Thursday evening we went to the Frolics, our own Divisional show.

Friday, 12th October.
I took the men detonating, and then went on with Sgt. Williams and Cpl. Mitchelmore to the line. Clegg of 182nd Brigade took me round and they gave me lunch afterwards at headquarters, rather a pleasant spot in a chalk pit near Fampoux. We ran down afterwards to the canal and just caught one of the motor boats which go up and down, and so got back quite easily in pouring rain by 4.30 p.m. We all went to the Spades before dinner.

Saturday, 13th October.
With Field to the cinema and tea at the Club ; then on to the Jocks, the 15th Division show, and quite good. Getting back at 10.30 from dinner at the Club I was told to go round to brigade. I went, struggling about a long way in the mud, to find it was all a mistake. Bed by 11.15 p.m.

Sunday, 14th October.
Up early with Field to Amiens. We dodged the French ticket authorities at both ends, getting out of the Gare du Nord at Amiens by a side door. We breakfasted at the Belfort, and then did some shopping. Lunch at the Godbert. The great difficulty about that place is that it is almost impossible not to over-eat. We separated till tea, when we met in a patisserie about 5 o'clock. We filled up a little time in an American bar, dined at 6.30 at the Godbert, and got back at 11 p.m. to hear we go up to the line to-morrow morning.

Monday, 15th October.
Started up at 10 a.m. and relieved by 2.30 p.m. in the right brigade sector, which seems easier to manage. It has turned very cold and we had some rain in the afternoon.

Tuesday, 16th October.
Nice morning. A large collection of Hun 'planes up. Field and Thacker came up in the morning and I went round with them. The Hun shelled a little in the night, getting one or two into Corona support near the dugout where we live.

Wednesday, 17th October.
Vacher and Sadler came up in the morning to look round. Not much to do in daylight. After dusk I worked for two hours with some men on an emplacement in Chemical trench. The Hun was using a great quantity of Very lights and a good deal of M.G. fire as if he expected something, though we had nothing ' on.'

Thursday, 18th October.
Some rain in the small hours, making the line very slippery, and movement unpleasant. I went round with Thacker in the morning, and fired three times during the day. While looking about near the far end of Corona I met the Corps Commander, Lt.-Gen. Ferguson, coming down Corfu Avenue. I had a working party digging an emplacement in some disused trenches at the end of Corona from 7-10 p.m.

Friday, 19th October.
Thacker up again, and another working party from 7-11.30 p.m. this time.

Saturday, 20th October.
I moved my headquarters across to the left side of the railway, to a dugout which is a Coy. headquarters of the 4th Glos., Heywood's Coy. I left the working party to itself to-night.

Sunday, 21st October.
Did not go out in the morning : rather tired. I don't like this sector, though really there is very little strafing. I went round the guns in the afternoon and came back to find a strafe from Thacker about the Corona emplacement, which should have been finished. I took the working party from 6-11 p.m. and finished it. Our guns were rather active, and at ten minutes past every hour the Hun sent a salvo of shells on to Corfu Avenue. I crept to bed very tired.

Monday, 22nd October.
Vacher relieved me this morning at 11 a.m. I had lunch at headquarters on my way down, and Thacker was very affable. I went back to the Q.M. stores by boat and dined at the Officers' Club. At 11 p.m. I went up to the station for the leave train, which was very crowded. There were eleven in my compartment.

Tuesday, 23rd October.
We reached Boulogne at 7 a.m. I went round to the Hotel Folkestone and had a wash and breakfast, then to the boat. Here I was told to come again next day, as my warrant was dated the 24th. I went away and wandered round the town, lunching at the Folkestone. Then, seeing the boat still there I went round again and saw the Duke of Connaught with one or two A.D.C.'s and Generals standing round. By keeping well under the eye of the A.M.L.O. and especially his Sergeant-Major I managed to get on board a second boat at about 6 o'clock, with a few others in the same case as myself. There was a good deal of difficulty getting off the boat as they seemed to have mislaid the gangway, and the comments of the men waiting on board were extremely funny, that one was being specially made, or the porters had gone home at trade union shutting-up time, &c., &c. Someone even offered the A.M.L.O. sixpence to go and buy a new one. We got off at last, however, amid tremendous cheers, and ran to the train. We snatched some seats originally meant for some P.N.O. people, who wished to turn us out. However we did not move and had an excellent dinner on the train. I shared a taxi with two others to the Langham, and got in by 10.30 p.m.

IV

Saturday, 3rd November.

I was called at 6 a.m. in the Grosvenor and met my travelling companion Wallace, of the 1st Camerons. We breakfasted comfortably in the train, and crossed at once. On the way some people fired a few rifle shots at something in the sea, which might have been a floating mine, but did not hit it. We reached Boulogne at 1 p.m., and at the enquiry office I found my train was not till 10 a.m. next day. Wallace and I then went to the Hotel Folkestone where I secured a bed. We lunched there, and then went out and did some shopping, had tea, and went to a cinema, where we saw pictures of the Zeppelin recently brought down in the south of France. We dined together in the hotel, a rather lengthy process, as they leave you so long between the courses. I left Wallace at 10.30 p.m. and went up to bed. He was going off by train at 12.50 a.m. up to Ypres. I never saw him again, but saw his name in the casualty list as killed somewhere about December 1st. I am very sorry as he was pleasant to meet, and a gentleman.

Sunday, 4th November.

I woke up in broad daylight to hear the newsboys shouting, and had a panic that I had overslept my train time : however I looked at my watch again and saw I was safe. I left Boulogne by the 10.57 a.m. train, which was very full, and as usual had but little glass in the windows. I tried in Boulogne to get a fur coat from an ordnance store, but could not. I travelled up with a fellow in the King's regiment recently come to Arras, a young captain with the M.C. We reached Arras at 5 p.m. and I went straight to the Officers' Club and stayed on for dinner. After that I went up to the battery Q.M. stores. Here I was handed an amazing note from Thacker, in which he said he had returned me to my battalion, accompanied by a long list of reasons, mostly to do with the Corona emplacement, and the detonating parties before. I spent the night in the store hut.

Monday, 5th November.

I started at 9.30 a.m. for the line, going to brigade headquarters first, even till then thinking it might be all a mistake, and Thacker be pulling my leg, it all seemed so extraordinary. In brigade I saw Foweraker, who is acting Brigade-Major. He greeted me with—" Hullo, Adams, I hear you have been dropping some bricks lately : come and talk it over," which was a very kind way of letting me down. He did talk it over pretty exhaustively, and advised me to keep clear of Thacker and generally wait

and see for a few days. A further and very salutary shock to my pride was given when I met Col. Bilton in the trench on my way to his headquarters. I said I was coming back to his battalion; to which he answered, "Yes, they asked me if I minded having you back, and I saw no reason for refusing to take you." He told me to go on to his headquarters and coming back himself a little later, was extremely kind, gave me lunch, and then handed me over to Eric Mitchell, who is commanding B company, my old company. Here I spent the rest of the day in a large gallery dugout. The company is in reserve, more than a thousand yards behind the front line, and not far from Fampoux. My servant Weeks turned up in the evening.

Tuesday, 6th November.
I stayed in all the morning, and in the afternoon took Weeks with me and went up to Cupid trench to see Field whom I knew to be there. I had a long talk with him, but he couldn't or wouldn't tell me much. I called on Perry and Wardrop (M.G.C.) on the way back, who were very nice, and went back later on and had a most delightful dinner with them, for which I was very grateful.

Wednesday, 7th November.
Rainy day. I went over to brigade in the morning and saw Foweraker again. He recommended me to wait and let things cool down, though I said I wanted to see the General and transfer at once to the machine gunners. I had a pleasant tea with Franklin of A company. Apparently I am to stay with B company, and as Mitchell is quite a good fellow I don't mind.

Thursday, 8th November.
Went out with Edge after breakfast to C company, living in Fampoux. Rain at lunch time. I took a working party out at 9.30 p.m. We struggled through the mud to the 7th Worcs. headquarters, where I saw Rowe. We had to wait there some time as the Hun was shelling Corfu pretty heavily. However things became quiet by 10 o'clock and we went up quite safely to Corona, where we had to do some clearing up; and also in the front line. We came away at 1 a.m., getting in at 2.30 a.m. without mishap. We hurried up a bit through Fampoux as our guns were just starting up for a raid by the division on our right.

Friday, 9th November.
Nothing to do in the morning. We were relieved at 2 p.m. Mitchell sent the company on ahead and he and I went down together. We picked up a lorry pretty soon, which took us into Arras. The billets are not bad : off the main street and near the theatre. Mitchell and I share a room, with beds but no sheets, next to the mess room. We dined at the Club, where I saw all the battery at a table together, and had rather a shock when he took me into the further room and introduced me to the whole six subalterns of the company, not one of whom I ever saw before.

Saturday, 10th November.
To the barracks with Mitchell in the morning, which is where the battalion are living. I am acting as second in command of the company.

I had a bath at the Club after lunch and dined there with Mitchell and Franklin. I can't settle down to my new brother officers very easily.

Sunday, 11th November.
Nothing to do in the morning. Out for a bit of a walk in the afternoon. Mitchell and I dined well at the Hotel de Commerce, the first time I have been there. O.C. Constable, old Marlburian, turned up off leave in the evening.

Monday, 12th November—Thursday, 15th November.
Work with the company in the mornings, once on the range in the moat of Vauban's fortifications. Mitchell and I dined out every night at the Club or the Hotel de Commerce, and went to a show, of which there are five now in Arras, and all pretty good.

Friday, 16th November.
A brigade shooting competition. I was on the range as an assistant to Foweraker, which more or less meant being O.C. range. It was rather dull and very cold. Mitchell and I went to the Follies (4th Division), and afterwards dined at the Commerce.

Saturday, 17th November.
On the range again with Foweraker—12 to 5 p.m. this time. The G.O.C. turned up, and quite a crowd of people. Mitchell and I dined at the Officers' Club, and then I saw him off at the station on his way to a Lewis gun course at Le Touquet. I am now in command of the company.

Sunday, 18th November.
Went to an early Celebration, and saw Vacher there. The G.O.C. inspected the barracks after church, and Tommy Coates, his A.D.C., invited me to dine. I went to A mess division at half past seven and was given a cocktail by Coates. Dinner was a little late. I sat on the General's left, with Col. Singleton opposite me. There were also there Col. Wake (G 1), and Anderson (G 2), Bevan, who was up at the House with me, and Coates. We had a most pleasant dinner and the General was very genial. All the ' G ' people went away afterwards, but Singleton and Coates stayed behind, and played the piano. The former produced some songs which he had written when in India and played them, while Coates sang. I played a little as well.

Monday, 19th November.
I watched the company beat D company at football in the morning, and spent from 1-3 with a working party, to my great annoyance as the subaltern who should have been there did not turn up. At half past three I went to a Company Commander's meeting and at the end the Colonel said he would put my name down for the next Vickers gun course, which comes off in February, if you please ! I dined at the Club with Cyril Holcroft.

Tuesday, 20th November.
This morning there was more football, the company beating C. In the evening there was a battalion concert, one of the worst I have ever been to. I did not stay long, coming away with Cyril Holcroft. We

dined again together and then went on to brigade headquarters, where we saw his brother Roy, Foweraker, and one or two others. Roy was trying to make out on the map the extent of the latest push at Cambrai. It seems to have been remarkably successful, and we finished up with quite an hilarious evening.

Wednesday, 21st November.
Rainy morning. We left the barracks at 2 p.m. and marched to Cam valley on the Fampoux road beyond the railway, where we had tea. From there, after a rather dismal wait, we went up to the front line, relieving 182 by 7.45. Mine is the right company of the left brigade sector, company headquarters being in a deep dugout in Charlie support, on the right of Costa. At 9 p.m. the right brigade raided, which brought a certain amount of retaliation upon us, but nothing very serious.

Thursday, 22nd November.
The Colonel came round in the morning. At midday the Hun began a little slow shelling, but did no damage. Fortunately he does not put T.M.'s on to this sector. At 3.30 p.m. I went down to battalion headquarters in Chili Avenue for a Company Commanders' meeting and stayed there till 6.30 p.m.

Friday, 23rd November—Monday, 26th November.
The usual trench routine. I went patrolling one night, for the first time in my life. Stallard came back on Sunday and took command of the company. He is very young, and seems rather to like the war.

Tuesday, 27th November.
I went out of the line in the morning with a few men to take over from the 7th Worcs. in support. We were nicely settled in when the relief was cancelled and so we had to go all the way back. What was worse I left my mackintosh in a dugout behind and could not find it when I went back to look for it. We had a very quiet night.

Wednesday, 28th November.
We were relieved early by the 15th Division and left the line at 11 a.m. They have twice as many men as we did and I cannot imagine where they will all go. We reached Arras at 4.30 p.m. and fixed ourselves up in a new billet not far from the Petite Place. I have a bed, and we have quite a good mess. I went down alone to the Officers' Club for dinner and found it full, so went on to the Commerce. There were one or two fresh ruins to see on the way as the Hun had been dropping some 14-inch shells into the town during the afternoon. Towards the end of my dinner I saw Wardrop at another table, and going across who should I see but Field, just come off leave, dining with the machine gunners. He and I stayed on talking and then we went to his mess, as the others were not yet out of the line, and finally he came over to our mess and sat quite a long time.

Thursday, 29th November.
I got up very late, went to the Field Cashier for money, and paid the company at 2.30 p.m. There was nothing to do besides that. I dined with Wardrop at the Club.

Friday, 30th November.

Up at 4.30 a.m., rather grizzly. We marched to Dainville and entrained there, reaching Bapaume at 11 a.m., where we got out. Marching a little way out of the town we halted in a field. On the way through I saw Major Hannay wearing an Army Staff armlet, one time Adjutant of the Inns of Court. On arrival at our halting place we were greeted with the reassuring news that the Hun had broken through and retaken most of the ground we had captured ten days before, if not a little extra, and we were to go up and stop him !

Presently a long fleet of motor buses came, a somewhat excited officer on Army Staff ran up and asked who we were and then told us to get in. We did, and drove off to Ruyaulcourt, where we got out again. Here we stayed half an hour. The road was crowded with men and transport coming back, especially machine gunners from the tanks. One officer we spoke to said the Hun had taken a lot of our guns and the whole of a Division. This was not true, as a matter of fact, though he very nearly did. Presently we moved on again, marching now, the road becoming more and more crowded as we went along. We went through a village called Metz, turned to the left, and presently found ourselves in a canvas camp in Havrincourt wood, on the right of the road, which we took over from the Grenadier Guards. They, after being in rest about three hours, had been called up in a hurry again that morning. We had our valises, luckily, and I shared a tent with Stallard, but did not undress beyond taking my boots off, as we were supposed to be ready to move at a moment's notice.

Saturday, 1st December.

A cold day. There was a big artillery strafe somewhere near during the morning, and various rumours kept coming in during the day. Apparently a good deal of the ground lost yesterday was regained this morning. We remained in our wood most of the day till 6 p.m. when we started for the line. The way led across the open, broad rolling ground with no track to go by. We saw the marks of many tanks which had gone over on Nov. 20th. Nearer Villers Pluich were signs of the other side of the story, artillery officers' valises complete, and ready to be rifled by the first person who came along. We reached Villers Pluich and halted at the railway level crossing, whereupon the Hun immediately began to shell, dropping some uncomfortably close. The men were given two extra bandoliers of ammunition each and we moved on again in single file up the hill to La Vacquerie. It was a most eerie journey, very little shelling, very dark, and I at least had no idea where we were ultimately going. La Vacquerie seemed very badly knocked about and no one was in it. Past that village we began to go down hill again along a slightly sunken road. I was expecting momentarily to run into a Bosch trench. Presently we passed C company installed in a trench : someone gave us a cheery good-night and we still went forward. About 2 a.m. we reached a trench —the support trench of the Hindenburg front system, dug very wide, and dry. From there we went forward up a communication trench, getting out at one point to cross a road, to a trench some six hundred yards further forward, and about midway between the Hindenburg front and

support systems. Here we took over from a mixed collection of Sherwoods, R.B.'s, &c., &c., out of two or three different divisions. There were two Vickers guns there, and these also relieved themselves. We finished this by 4 a.m., and established posts along the line.

Sunday, 2nd December.
At 6 a.m. Stallard sent me back to the support line, the original support line of the Hindenburg front system, as he had too many officers up in front. It was now more or less daylight. I left my equipment, including compass, glasses, and haversack, in the front line dugout. Back in the support line I found Cyril Holcroft, and we both lay down to sleep. Unfortunately I had forgotten to take any food back with me, though I had my water bottle and my pack with my washing and shaving kit in it, for which I was afterwards very thankful. We were both sleeping peacefully at 2.30 p.m. or about then, when someone shouted down the dugout steps that the Huns were coming. I took my pack and water bottle with me, and we both went upstairs to see what was happening. Things seemed rather confused, though there was not much shelling. We found our left flank entirely unguarded—' in the air ' as they say—and soon a message came along to say that the people on the right had fallen back behind us; so Cyril decided we had better go too, which we did, up a communication trench to the Hindenburg front line. Here we found a mixed multitude of Sherwoods, Gloucesters, R.B.'s, &c., none of whom had any ammunition or bombs to speak of. We could see across a slight dip in the ground to where our front line had been in the morning, and even see some Bosches once or twice. Stallard came in, hit in two or three places, and did not know what had become of any of the others. He went on behind to be dressed. By 5 p.m. the Bosch seemed to be getting decidedly the best of it, and we began to wonder who was behind us. Cyril sent my namesake over to the sunken road on our right rear, with a few men, to see we were not cut off, and then I went back with one or two men and Brown of A company to Mitchell's trench, some three or four hundred yards behind. This was quite unpleasant, as it was quite light still, and we had to get through a good deal of wire, and there was a good deal of M.G. fire at the time. However we found Mitchell at last and how many men he had got with him. I stayed till it was dark, about six o'clock, and then went forward again with Brown to Holcroft, nearly falling into a large and watery shell hole on the way. Cyril we found with a Sherwood captain who luckily was still on the 'phone to his battalion : however they were quite pleased at our news. At 10 p.m., since things seemed to have quieted down, a patrol was sent under 2/Lt. Jackson (8th Worcs.) into the trench in front. He returned to say it was unoccupied, so we all went forward again and held it. To my great joy I found my trench coat still in the dugout where I had left it. Apparently the Bosch had not been downstairs, but he had made little dumps of stick, grenades and egg bombs all along the trench which we put ready for our own use. We established a bombing block on the right, as the Bosch was found to be in the extreme end of the trench next to the sunken road.

About midnight some 5th Warwicks came up to relieve us; however they had managed to lose half their company by the way. We sent off

as many men as we could, under the three remaining subalterns and Cyril and I stayed on. 2/Lt. Martin had not been seen or heard of since the beginning of the attack, and was presumably killed or a prisoner. I had had nothing to eat except a few sardines since the day before, and it was bitterly cold; however I found, lying in the trench, a fur jerkin which I put on under my trench coat, and walked up and down, and still shivered.

Monday, 3rd December.
The rest of the Warwicks came along at 6 a.m., by which time it was almost getting light. We bundled them into their positions and scrambled out as best we could up the communication trench, and then along the Hindenburg front line to another sunken road on the left. We were obviously in sight, because they turned machine guns on to us once or twice, but without effect. At last, about 7 a.m., in broad daylight, we reached "Corner Work," a kind of redoubt, where was the battalion headquarters of the 5th Warwicks. We put our men, the remains of A and B companies, into a dugout in the side of the road with D company, and I told them they could eat their iron rations. Then I went into Col. Coates' dugout and lay down on the floor by Holcroft to sleep. At 8.15 a.m. the Hun began another heavy barrage, and presently Major Wyatt of the 4th Gloucesters came down to say that his battalion had retired from their position on the right in front of La Vacquerie. This time our left seemed fairly secure, though I don't know who was there. Wyatt saw me and sent me outside to find out what was happening. Without going very far I could see the Bosche in La Vacquerie and already past our position. I reported this, and they all came up then, and the men "stood to." After that, for the next hour, life was pretty strenuous. The shelling had stopped, as the Bosche was too close to us. However before long he was throwing hand grenades and sniping from a trench parallel to and *behind* ours, and there seemed no particular reason why he should not surround us completely. Col. Coates and Cyril solemnly burnt their maps and orders, a proceeding which seems humorous to look back upon, but which was not at all so at the time. The Colonel then decided that the place was too hot to hold—we had had a fair number of casualties, including Sgt.-Major Tarrant of B company killed—and so we cleared out to the left and lined the bank of the road, at that point sunken only on the one side. The Bosch immediately occupied the trenches we had left and began throwing bombs at us from there. Obviously we could not stay out in the open there, so we swung back into a good but wide trench facing our original front, continuing another running out of Corner Work. By this time it was about 10 a.m. The Bosche seemed content with what he had done, and we sat down in comparative peace, except that, so far as we knew there was no one on either flank and no means of going back except over the open; not that we were thinking of going back just then. The N.C.O.'s and men were behaving splendidly. No one seemed to be in the least disturbed, which was fortunate, as that sort of thing is so infectious. The trench we were in was very wide, and so the men scraped little recesses for themselves to sit in; and there was also a good triple entranced dugout, in which we put some wounded, but no one else. Cpl. King had a Lewis gun at the right hand end of the

trench next to Corner Work, facing down the road, and there was a bombing post there as well, facing the work. Then, about 2 p.m., Jackson of B company came into the trench to say he had brought up a fair number of men and had them all in a trench behind. These had been sent up by Col. Coates, who had gone back to collect some. I suppose the Hun saw them coming, for from 2.30 to 3.30 he gave us a most tremendous dusting down with every gun he could lay hands on, and uncommonly accurate shooting too. We had a further twenty casualties or so from this, who went down into the dugout. The rest had to stay up as, considering the bombardment, we expected him to come over any minute. He seemed to have withdrawn from Corner Work as he was sending up lights directing the barrage from behind it. By four o'clock things had quieted down a bit, and by six he had quite stopped. Then, under cover of darkness one or two men went forward to get some wounded out of a dugout further down the road towards the Bosche. They managed to bring back a few men, though stretcher cases they had to leave. I arranged sentry groups and reliefs along the trench and sent all the spare men down below to keep warm. There were two other officers besides Cyril and we took it in turns to keep watch, an hour at a time.

Tuesday, 4th December.

At 3 a.m. some 184 people came up to relieve us and we staggered out along the remains of what had been a communication trench, and then along the old British front line to the road leading to Villers Pluich, across this and into Farm Ravine, where our battalion headquarters was. The men were put into a shelter for the night and given some rations—the first for forty-eight hours. We—the four subalterns—shared a small shelter, where I dumped all my kit, and then went up to headquarters for some food. We were given some most delightful machonochie. However in the middle of this someone shouted "gas," and I found I had left my respirator down with my other kit. I ran down to get it, some little way, and then came back and finished my dinner. Then we went down to the shelter again and slept. At 6.0 a.m., after a couple of hours sleep, we had to stand to for a Bosch barrage. By this time I, and the others too, were not in the rudest of health and spirits. I put B company, such as it was, into a trench near by, and got some food for them. I met a man of the 183 M.G.'s who said he thought all the officers were killed, but this was not in the least true; I think Smith, a thoroughly good fellow, was the only one killed, though Perry was taken prisoner. Then I shaved, which was a great comfort. I went up to battalion headquarters again for something and on the way met Field, who greeted me with "Hullo, George; I thought you were dead." I rested most of the day until 7.0 p.m., when I took the company up to the old British support line, and handed over command to O. C. Constable, who was there with the party Holcroft had sent out of the Hindenburg line two nights before when the first half company of Warwicks appeared. Here we spent the night.

Wednesday, 5th December.

Constable and I were together in a shelter and were roused at about 3 a.m. I think, pretty early anyhow, by a Bosch barrage on our front line. This lasted about half an hour and was repeated three times up to 8.0 a.m.

We were in communication by telephone with Mitchell, who was in front all the time and he seemed to be undisturbed by it. I felt most awfully ill and could not eat or do anything, so I simply lay about the trench and tried to rest. In the afternoon we changed over to a slightly larger shelter. At 1 a.m. we were relieved by the Berks, whom we were most profoundly glad to see. Constable had gone on ahead somewhere, so I took the company out. Jackson had reconnoitred a way across country which avoided most of Villers Pluich, and he led the way. Most of us could only just stagger along. I left a rather nice water-bottle up there which I never saw again.

Thursday, 6th December.

We reached Havrincourt wood at 4 a.m. and were put into some tents. When it was day I went and saw the doctor, the same American whom I had met first at Ypres, and he told me I was gassed by the fact that I had a kind of sore rash round my mouth and nose. I then went to bed again.

Friday, 7th December—Saturday, 8th December.

Friday I spent in bed. Saturday afternoon I had to get up, as the Brigadier, Spooner, came along and spoke to the battalion, congratulating us on what we had done.

Sunday, 9th December.

We were inspected in the morning by Gen. Mackenzie : I thought I should drop every moment. He seemed very pleased about something, though he said we should have to go into the line again. During his inspection the Hun began to shell our camp in the wood with instantaneous bursting 4.2's, and at the same time it began to rain hard. We were not allowed to go into the camp for coats and had to wander about in the rain getting wetter and wetter. In about an hour and a half the Hun stopped and I went back to bed.

Monday, 10th December.

Weeks, my servant since Tidworth, went sick this morning and was removed to hospital. I took on a man called Weyman, a born fool, guaranteed to lose an officer's kit complete in three days. They told me I was to go back to transport lines for a few days to get right again. So at 2.15 p.m. I started out with about seventy men. With me came the Padre, Wainwright, of St. Matthew's, Westminster, Tetlow and two other officers. We were half way to Metz when the Hun began to shell the road in front, getting one direct hit and killing a mule : so we waited twenty minutes and let him cool down. We came through safely and pushed on across country to Equancourt ; the Padre walking with me and talking very pleasantly. I had hardly met him before. In the end we settled down on the floor of a Nissen hut, ate some food the Q.M. gave us, and slept.

Tuesday, 11th December.

We had a table, benches, and three wire beds made by the pioneers, one bed coming to my use. This made things much more comfortable. I spent most of the day in my bed.

EQUANCOURT—BRAY

Wednesday, 12th December—Friday, 21st December.

I stayed back at Equancourt all this time, doing very little. At first I found a walk of two hundred yards made me wish to sit down and die, but I soon got over that. The Colonel came and dined one evening; and one morning, meeting him in the street, he told me that he had recommended my name for a Military Cross. Cyril Holcroft's has gone in for a D.S.O., which he well deserves. Constable came down for a time, and the T.M.'s had their reserve officer close to us, who was Vacher part of the time. He lived with a pioneer officer, by name Hainsselin, who had been in the Navy and was altogether a rather refreshing person. I discussed many things also with the Padre, mainly based on Rugby and Trinity, Cambridge, on the one side, and Marlborough and the House on the other. He forms an agreeable contrast. For the last two or three days we had all the T.M.'s, including Thacker, sleeping in the hut : a momentary embarrassment. I saw a good deal of Field and Vacher.

Saturday, 22nd December.

By this time I was quite fairly strong again, and walked over to Manancourt to prospect for billets for the battalion. I found that rather a long trip, however, as I had not tried anything quite so adventurous before.

Sunday, 23rd December.

We moved over to Manancourt at about midday, to another Nissen hut, shared with C company. I had a bed, and my thick pyjamas came in a parcel brought by the battalion, who came in at 4 p.m., so I was very comfortable.

Monday, 24th December.

Hard frost, with slight rain on the top of it, making the roads like glass. We had little to do all day till 5.30 p.m., when we marched to a railhead near by and entrained, officers in cattle trucks. We went by train to the Plateau station and marched from there to Bray-sur-Somme, total distance from Manancourt about twenty miles. The march from the Plateau station was a very hazardous and slippery performance. Most of the battalion fell down " not once nor twice." We were settled in, I on a wire bed, by 1 a.m.

Tuesday, 25th December. Christmas Day.

Nothing much to do. I went round the company in the morning : they had a sort of preliminary blow out in the form of a beer ration and some extra meat. I saw Field for a moment in the street. Just before lunch the Colonel came into the billet and congratulated Holcroft on his D.S.O., and then turned to me and told me I was given an M.C., which is very pleasant news. In the evening the officers had a battalion dinner. I had the luck to sit next to Major Davies, with Holcroft close by, and we had a delightful time.

Wednesday, 26th December.

I walked out a little in the morning. We had some more snow during the day. In the evening we had a duck for dinner, and generally rather spread ourselves. B company mess in a room alone now instead of the original idea of three companies together. Holcroft could not stand that

either and moved to another house. The company mess consists of myself, Gale, and Jackson. Both were studying to be architects a year or two ago.

Thursday, 27th December.
On parade this morning 9-1, and bitterly cold it was. Churchill, the Brigade-Major, came up and told me we were only staying here a few days, though anyhow we shall not go up the line for some little time, I fancy. Field and Vacher came in after tea and sat talking for some little time, and invited me in to dinner on Saturday—Thacker being on leave.

Friday, 28th December.
By the Adjutant's kindness I went into Amiens by myself, starting on a lorry at 9 a.m. and getting in at 11.45 after a good drive along the Amiens-Vermand road. I went to the American bar and fortified myself with one or two cocktails: then lunch at the Godbert. After that I had my hair cut and went out on a tram to Mentières to the wholesale canteen to order a gramophone for H.Q. mess. Coming back I had a magnificent bath at the Belfort, which lasted till half past five. Another visit to the American bar, and then dinner in the Godbert with some D.C.L.I. people out of our own pioneer battalion. I gave them a lift back in my lorry, which had also brought a sergeant to buy food for the men's Christmas dinner. By the time we came out of dinner snow was an inch or two deep on the roads, and was continuing to fall. The driver did not want to start at all, but we said we must go back and so we pushed off. We managed the long hill up to the Vermand road without any mishap and then, about two hundred yards beyond the turning, we stuck in a drift. We were not the only ones, for there were three lorries in front, including one with double drive, i.e. driving power to all four wheels. We all got out and scraped away the snow and pushed behind till at last the lorry moved forward with a jerk and we had to run for some way to keep up. However it soon stuck again, and the process was repeated. After the eighth or ninth time the driver and one or two of the passengers began to lose heart and craved for the warmth of Amiens: however I said we must go on and the leader of the D.C.L.I. party backed me up, so we continued our efforts. Shortly afterwards a car passed us travelling from the east and we learnt from them that the drifts only lasted for another two hundred yards. One of the others came forward with me to verify this, and we were just turning back having decided that the man was lying when a lorry swept past which turned out to be ours. We got in then, and never stopped involuntarily again. A snow plough had been along the road beyond Villers Bretonneux, so going was quite easy. We reached Bray by 1 a.m.

Saturday, 29th December.
Parade in the morning as before. I dined with the T.M.'s, Thacker being away, and had a very jolly time.

Sunday, 30th December.
Church parade at 10 a.m. in a smallish room, where we had to stand all the time. The brigade band was there and gave some support to the

hymns. The men had their Christmas dinner at 1.30 p.m.—roast meat, plum pudding, and beer—which they seemed to enjoy. The Colonel came round and wished them all a happy Christmas, or New Year, I suppose it was. Cpl. King was wearing a bit of D.C.M. ribbon for his work at La Vacquerie.

Monday, 31st December.

We moved, marching, to Bayonvillers, on the south side of the Vermand road. Going was very slippery, but it was only eight or nine miles in all. We got there by 1 p.m. into first-class billets. I have a bed with sheets in a room to myself, and the mess is in the same house. Jackson and Gale, the only others in the company, are quite respectable people on closer acquaintance.

Col. Bilton met me in the street and told me my name had gone in for the M.G.C. Apparently they wanted it in a hurry, asking for names by wire.

Tuesday, 1st January—Saturday, 5th January, 1918.

We had some more snow on the first. The other days we did company training on the north side of the Vermand road, mostly in fairly deep snow. Near a small piece of trench there I found the grave of a French soldier, dated 28th of August, 1914. That sets one thinking.

Sunday, 6th January.

We had a church parade this morning standing in a barn in a perfectly Arctic atmosphere. Luckily it did not last long. It was the day of prayer commanded to be observed by the King, and his proclamation was read. In the afternoon I walked over the snow to Marcelcave and saw Field and Vacher. Mortimer was there when I arrived. I only stayed a short time, and Field walked a little way back with me. He told me that Cpl. Impey was killed by a whizz-bang quite close to him during the second tour up in front of La Vacquerie, when I was at Equancourt. In the evening there descended upon us a big reinforcement draft

Monday, 7th January.

Up at 6.30 a.m. At 8.15 we started for Carrèpuits, beyond Roye about eighteen miles in all. The new draft came on parade, a most amazing crowd of ruffians wearing their great coats and equipment slung round them like the picture of the White Knight. I rode part of the way, under pressure from Davies. We went part of the way along the same road that I had come when marching the battery back from Nesle to Villers Bocage ages before. We ran into a rather heavy snowstorm and all got properly wet. Jackson, Gale and I shared a room at the end, and I had a bed, but no sheets. The men are all together in a large French hut.

Tuesday, 8th January—Wednesday, 9th January.

Battalion parade each morning, after which we had the men to ourselves. I inspected my draft like a roving Major-General, and told them how to dress themselves, &c.: rather amusing. The score of Elgar's First Symphony came, a present from Mia, and is most interesting.

Thursday, 10th January.
A big thaw this morning, making everything very wet and clammy. I went over to a French Flying Squadron near by, one of whose officers I had met yesterday, and asked him to take me up, but he said there was too much wind. He gave me a drink of " Porto " in his canteen, which I did not much care about, and then we parted.

Friday, 11th January.
We started at 11.30 a.m. and marched to Voyennes on the Somme, about ten miles. I rode part of the way again. We were leading company this time, and Holcroft was commanding the battalion, as Davies was elsewhere, so I rode with him. The country beyond Nesle began to be familiar—Voyennes is only two miles from Bethencourt, where we were in March last year. We arrived at 3.15 p.m. in pelting rain, to find Rundle, who had gone sick from Cambrai, and three new officers waiting for us. Of these, two have been out before, and one not. I had a bed with sheets.

Saturday, 12th January.
Battalion parade at 10 a.m. We did some drill, and then turned the new subalterns on to their platoons. Nothing much to do after lunch. We had more snow in the night.

Sunday, 13th January.
We left at 9.30 a.m. and marched to Vaux, through Foreste and Germaine, where we lived once before. It was rather a tiring march and I did not ride much of the way. We found excellent French huts at the end : all the men in one, and the officers in another, divided up into cubicles for one or two. I had one alone. My servant shone very much here—not Weyman now, but Day, who is really Constable's batman when he is here—dashing about as soon as we got in and getting me a basin to wash in, a fire, and food for the mess. We also have a real Frenchman as a cook, a man who came up in the last draft. He says he was a chef at the Berkeley Hotel, but, judging by his appearance, Davies thinks he was more probably a bottle washer.

Monday, 14th January.
It snowed hard all the morning so we had no parade. I lectured to the N.C.O.'s on map reading, a pet subject of mine, and one they know little about. In the afternoon I went a walk with Jackson and we did a little souveniring of bedroom furniture which we found among the ruins of the houses round about.

Tuesday, 15th January.
Cold and rainy. We employed ourselves in the morning doing a ' platoon attack,' to everyone's satisfaction.

Wednesday, 16th January.
We were to have done a battalion attack this morning, and did get out on to the ground ready to begin when such a storm of rain came on that it had to be abandoned. In the afternoon I went over in the gig to Foreste for money, and saw Vacher there, just going on leave. I walked back.

Thursday, 17th January.

Rain all day. I dined at battalion and had oysters, and spent quite a jolly and delightful evening.

Friday, 18th January.

An inspection parade at 10 a.m. Rundle took the company, as I was in the special character of " recipient." Gen. Mackenzie came along and presented us all with our ribbons, and also a little paper saying what we had done. He shook hands with each of us, and said to me : " Is this what you left the T.M.'s for ? " Surely he knew why I left them. Then we stood in a row behind him, while the battalion marched past.

At 4.30 p.m. we started for the line, up to a big dugout in a railway cutting on the west side of Savy wood. This dugout has about sixteen entrances leading down from the railway track, which is in a cutting here, to a long passage from which branch out rooms at intervals. The five officers, myself among them, all slept together in a small room on one side and ate in a larger one just opposite. We shared the main dugout with C company, but their officers slept on top.

Saturday, 19th January.

I went out this morning with Rundle round the Brown line, an half constructed defence system round Manchester Hill. We saw St. Quentin again well. The spire of the Cathedral has been pushed down since we were here last. In the afternoon I went out again by myself with a compass looking about. This is a most delightful sector : hardly a shell a day, and the weather so far good.

Sunday, 20th January.

Nothing much to do. I spent some more time trying to make a sketch map of the wire and trenches round Manchester Hill and Francilly. Some magnificent Zeiss glasses came for me, lent by Mr. Cherry. Some rain in the evening.

Monday, 21st January.

Rain all the morning. I went over to the support company of the 7th Worcs. in the Bois des Roses, looking across a little valley to the Selency-St. Quentin road. It was pretty muddy going. I found Leck there too : he lives next door to the infantry company.

Tuesday, 22nd January.

Nothing to do during the day. At dusk we moved up to the support company headquarters and settled in, dining with the M.G.'s : in fact we mess together always, which is rather jolly. I went out afterwards with No. 8 platoon—my old crowd—digging in a resistance line near the forward company headquarters further down this valley. There are several of the old ones left—Halford, Williams, White, Jones, and a small boy called Filer, who looks about sixteen and seems quite to have become an " old hand." Everything was very quiet.

Wednesday, 23rd January.

I went out with Leck at 6.45 a.m. and round the line of resistance to the various company headquarters. We got back by 8.15 just as it was light, having called at Battalion in Francilly on the way. That is

just the sort of life I like, wandering freely over a mile or two of country, instead of being cooped up in two hundred yards of stinking trench. I did not go out again till after dark: for one thing they try to keep down movement as much as possible. After dinner I went down and called on D company, in front, and then went on by myself to the other companies, getting back from A company, somewhere on the forward slope of Manchester Hill, by 12.30 a.m.

Thursday, 24th January.
Got up fairly late, and had nothing to do before lunch. At 3 p.m. I went to Battalion for a meeting, and then, after dinner, Leck, Fryer, his second in command, and I went up to Fayet to see Field. We were very jovial, and sang and laughed a good deal on the way there and back. I wish I could get into the 183rd M.G. company.

Friday, 25th January.
I went out this morning with Rundle through Francilly on to the forward side of Manchester Hill. It was a gloriously fine day, and very clear indeed. I had Mr. Cherry's glasses with me and had a good look at the Rocourt salient, which I believe the French had a go at, some time back. Certainly it seems blown to blazes, and there are some enormous shell holes there. We moved back along a ravine and then sat on the Roman road for some time looking at St. Quentin, and watching some air fights. The odd thing is that one never sees a Bosch, though the town is crammed with them. Franklin came back from in front before dinner, as he said "to get a rest from his subalterns." I feel the same need too, sometimes. Later on I went down with him and Holcroft to his front line posts. The left post—close to the Fayet-St. Quentin road—is not a good place, and the approach, a shallow trench, is two feet deep in mud.

Saturday, 26th January.
Quiet morning. A heavy fog hung about all day, limiting observation to about 200 yards. At 5.30 p.m. we were relieved by the 7th again and went back to the same dugout in Savy wood.

Sunday, 27th January—Tuesday, 29th January.
We rather expected something on the Sunday, being the Kaiser's birthday, but nothing unusual occurred. The company worked by night on the Brown line, and by day I wandered about by myself making sketch maps and generally spying out the land.

Wednesday, 30th January.
A lovely morning and very quiet. At 5.30 p.m. we left our dugout and went up to take over from the left front company, D company and ourselves changing places, from last time. I went up at 8 p.m. with 2/Lt. Parker, and took a few men out on patrol in No Man's land, a thing I had hardly ever done before. We wandered about pretending to see things and finding them after all to be bushes or stumps. After about two hours we came in by the left hand post. Then I went round the posts, getting back by 1 a.m. Everything is very quiet except the machine guns, which he occasionally turns on to the roads.

ST. QUENTIN—HOLNON WOOD

Thursday, 31st January.

I went round my posts at 6.0 a.m. with Davies, on to C company's left post and thence down the Roman road, in by 9.0 a.m. Luckily there was a bit of a mist, or we should have been caught by the daylight, as most of these posts are in view of the Hun. In the afternoon I went across to Fig wood by Fayet, and called on Richards, the M.G., who is in charge of some guns up there. I went back and dined with Leck and D company, and had oysters. It was perhaps a trifle risky, but since things are so quiet here one can afford to do things one would not elsewhere.

Friday, 1st February.

Mist all day. I went round the posts at 5 a.m., taking the Sgt.-Major with me. The morning seems the best time to go as the Bosch is generally sleepy, and keeps his machine guns quiet. I did not go out again much until the evening. We had to shift down to the right one post, giving up our worst one to the Gloucesters and taking two from C company astride the Roman road. Also I was relieving the men in the posts, so altogether the manœuvre was a rather complicated one. After most careful instructions at last everyone found their places and settled down. Then at 9.30 p.m. a damn fool of a Gloucester officer came in to say he couldn't find his own post, and would I give him a guide. I was just going up then myself, and so I took him up to No. 7 post near the crater on the Selency road and told him to follow the trench, sending two men with him, so that they also should know the way. Then I went on round the posts and back. The two new ones, one on the Roman road and one two hundred yards away to the right can be reached by daylight, as I had been up to them during the afternoon with the two corporals who were to take over.

Saturday, 2nd February.

A glorious day. I got up fairly late. After lunch I went outside and sat on the grass on my groundsheet with a book until disturbed by the first shell that had come near us during our whole tour in. They put over about half a dozen 4.2's in all, but did no damage. At tea time in walked Eric Mitchell, having come back from Monte Carlo, where he was sent after a go of trench fever. An extra officer from the Bucks came up too, to take over to-morrow, and so we were fairly crowded.

Sunday, 3rd February.

Round the posts early with Mitchell. Quiet day. We were relieved in the evening by the Bucks, who got in without any mishap. Mitchell and I stayed till all the company were clear, and then walked out together. I felt most awfully tired, though I hadn't done so very much. We went through Holnon to the far side of Holnon wood, where we found huts for ourselves, not far from Attilly. Mitchell and I share a cubicle in a joint hut for A and B companies.

Monday, 4th February.

Breakfast in bed. Did nothing in the morning. After lunch I went out with Mitchell reconnoitring the digging ground on the high land south of Maissemy. Corps say the Bosch will push here, and so we have to dig a big defensive system.

1918

Tuesday, 5th February.

I went over to Forestc this morning by lorry and saw Foweraker about my transfer. Apparently it has not been stopped by Division and so has probably gone right through. In that case the only thing to do is to be patient with hope. I came back by the return leave bus through Beauvois and Villevecque. Hateful as our time was in some ways when we were there before I found myself wanting to get out and look about, and particularly to go and see if anything was left of our bivouac under the lee of a certain brick wall.

Wednesday, 6th February.

With the company digging in the morning, up above Fresnoy. In the afternoon there was a brigade parade, and Spooner bade farewell to the 7th Worcesters, who are being disbanded, on this new system of three battalions to a brigade. About forty of them came to B company, with one officer. Among the men was Pte. Hunt, who used to be a shining light in No. 5 platoon in old days, and for a time was Symons' servant at Brentwood. He is quite an acquisition.

Thursday, 7th February.

Out again digging. We get a fine view from these trenches, and can see rows of camouflage screens put up by the Bosch along one of his roads. We actually saw some men as well. Back by lunch time. My servant, Weeks, turned up again from hospital, for which I am very glad. I had a very cheery letter from Ffooks in Salonika congratulating me on my M.C. of which I told him in a letter dated Christmas Day.

Friday, 8th February—Saturday, 9th February.

I stayed in on Friday with Mitchell settling up the company and arranging about the new men. Saturday I went out digging again. We had oysters for dinner, it being my birthday, but no post, which was rather disappointing.

Sunday, 10th February.

In the morning I walked very pleasantly across country to Beauvois to see Field. The servants told me he had gone yesterday morning to the 5th Manchesters—his old battalion—as there wasn't room for two captains in the battery, and his third star had come through. That was quite natural and to be expected, but apparently at 5 p.m. the same day Thacker's Indian Army transfer came through as well, which throws a different light on things. However it is not my business. I did not go into their mess and got a lift back, instead, to Marteville in an A.S.C. car, walking the rest of the way along the railway.

Monday, 11th February.

Out with Mitchell this morning round the digging ground. We came back through Maissemy and had quite a pleasant walk. After dinner we played bridge. About 11 o'clock the Adjutant rang me up to say that my transfer to the M.G.C. had come through, and I was to report myself at Grantham on the 20th. This caused some little excitement.

Tuesday, 12th February.

A misty morning. I walked up to Keeper's lodge with Mitchell, and saw Rawlings the R.E. Then on round the digging posts and back. I saw the Adjutant at lunch time and he said I could get away as soon as I liked. The midnight train to-night would be rather a scramble, so I shall go to-morrow afternoon. Franklin came in to tea, and he, Mitchell and I had quite an amusing time together. Bridge again after dinner.

Wednesday, 13th February.

Very wet. Packed up in the morning and said goodbye to Major Davies and one or two others, including my servant Weeks, whom I should have liked to take with me. I left at 2 p.m. in the gig and drove to Foreste, where I found the train. Thacker was there, going back for the Indian Army. I also saw Thompson of the 7th Worcs., not going by train. We had to change at Chaulnes, a most deadly place now, though I managed to get some tea there. Amiens at 8.45 p.m., after spending two hours on the way there from Villers Bretonneux, distance about five miles. I went to the Godbert and managed to get some sole and chicken before they closed down. After that I went to a very dull Officers' Club and sat reading some Macaulay I had with me.

Thursday, 14th February.

I caught the 12.16 a.m. Paris to Boulogne express. The train was very full, but I got a seat in a 1st, one of the Internationale Compagnie carriages, and comfortable enough for me to go to sleep from time to time, waking up finally at Boulogne at 5 a.m. I put my valise in the Consigne and went over to the new Officers' Club. This seems to be an excellent place. I had a wash and shave and something to eat and then wandered round the town. In the Club I met a fellow who was in my section in the Inns of Court O.T.C., though I cannot remember his name. I went to the quay at 8 a.m. and presented my warrant, 'duty' this time, and was told I could not go on the morning boat, but must come again at 2 p.m. This was rather a bore. However I went round to the Hotel Folkestone and had my boots cleaned, wandered in the town again and came back to the Folkestone for lunch. I embarked at about 2.30 p.m. and the boat started at 4, with a smooth sea; but it was misty and we could not see much. The train got in at Victoria at 8.30 p.m., and after trying the Great Western Hotel and the Langham, both of which were full, I laid myself down in the Bentinck, feeling thankful that I should probably not see France again for three months.

V

Saturday, 25th May, 1918.

I left the Savoy with Heathcock, accompanied by his friend Early-Smith, getting to Victoria at 7.30 a.m. We had rather a struggle to get a taxi at that early hour and finally went to the station driven by a woman in a Red Cross car. We got away by 7.50 and had breakfast on the train. At Folkestone we waited four hours, during which time we went up to the town and bought Italian phrase-books, &c. The sea was very calm in spite of a good breeze and we reached Boulogne at 5 p.m., and were told by the A.M.L.O. to go to Camiers. We saw to our valises, had tea in the Hotel du Louvre, and went on by train at 7.45 p.m., reaching Camiers in daylight. There the authorities said they knew nothing about us, and added the rather staggering announcement that " people never went to Italy from there." Finally we went to bed in tents, Heathcock, I, and two others : rather a strong contrast to the Savoy.

Trinity Sunday, 26th May.

There are twelve officers here all hoping to go to Italy, and we all reported in a body to the Adjutant at 9.30 a.m. He still knew nothing, but was wiring to find out from D.A.G. Heathcock and I, and Wall, another man from Grantham of our party, walked down to the sea through the sand dunes and watched some men bathing. We lunched at an inn called, in English, the " King's Manor," in front of a pretty lake. I believe Henry VIII. stayed here before or after the Field of the Cloth of Gold. We went to the sea again afterwards and had tea at a little estaminet near the shore. There are a good many pretty flowers about, and a fine Wistaria growing over one wing of the King's Manor.

Monday, 27th May.

This morning they put us through exactly the same gas tests as at Grantham, and then at 11 a.m. we were finished for the day. After lunch I went off with the other two to Etaples, where we managed to get some money from the Field Cashier. We had tea and dinner at an excellent Officers' Club there, put up as a memorial to two officers. Coming out we were rather amused by a private standing by the side of the road with his identity disc as a monocle, having had possibly one or even two ' extra glasses,' and asking rather petulantly, " Where's my blooming car ? " We got a lift back in a lorry.

Tuesday, 28th May.

Reporting in the morning to O.C. Reinforcements we were told to come again at 2 o'clock, and so went down to the sea. After lunch we went to the office again and were given our movement orders for Italy. The

first stage was Havre. We left Camiers at 6 p.m. by lorry and drove to Etaples. There we saw Lovell and Hunt, both from our squad at Grantham, who had crossed a day later than we did. They saw us off at 10.0 p.m. at the station—themselves having been detailed for the 9th Division. The train was fairly full, but Heathcock and I had corners, with Wall in the same compartment.

Wednesday, 29th May.
When dawn broke we were not far on our way. The train went slower even than most troop trains : we had rumours of a new Bosch attack which may have accounted for some of it. About six o'clock we stopped in a cutting and stayed there nearly two hours : we could see three other trains on the same line immediately in front of us and one behind. I walked up to the engine and got a mug full of hot water from the engine driver in which I shaved. We staved off the pangs of hunger with a tin of biscuits Heathcock had bought in Camiers. At 11.30 a.m. we reached Romescamps and stayed there two hours more. Nearly everyone got out and we were able to eat at a Y.M.C.A. place. After Romescamps we moved on a little faster and reached Havre at 9 p.m. Here Beevor, who took upon himself the direction of affairs, went to the Town Major to see about rooms ; and finally, dumping our valises at the big quayside stationyard, we walked, as there were no trams so late, to the Officers' Club in the middle of the town. There were five of us in a kind of dormitory, but we each had a bed with sheets and it was really very comfortable

Thursday, 30th May.
Wall and I went out in the morning looking about. We each had a bath and a shampoo and were horrified to see how filthy we had become in a few hours travelling. After lunch in the Club we three went over to the quayside station and saw to our valises. Dinner again at the Club, and then to the Gare des Voyageurs. This time the train was nearly empty. We left at 9 p.m. and slept nearly all the way.

Friday, 31st May.
We arrived in Paris at 5.30 a.m. Everyone seemed up and about, and so after leaving our valises in a safe place we had no difficulty in getting a taxi. We drove to an address given us of an Officers' Club, but could not find it, and after a good long drive round we discovered an hotel taken over by the Y.M.C.A., where we washed and had breakfast. Then we went to the Gare de Lyons, where we reported to the R.T.O. Our train left at 8 p.m., he told us, and we were free till then. Heathcock, Wall, and I kept together and walked out. We went to the Place de l'Opera, and looked at the diamonds in the Rue de la Paix : then down the Rue Rivoli, stopping for an ice at Rumpelmayers. The Louvre and the Luxembourg were both shut, so we could see nothing there, and walked instead up to the Bois de Boulogne, where we sat some time watching the people. We lunched well at the Hotel Westminster, and afterwards Wall and I went out again. Heathcock stayed in the Hotel and, I believe, went to sleep. For tea we had been advised to go to the Soldiers' Rest House in the Place Vendome, opposite the Bristol. We went, and found we were rather mistaken, as the place was really only

meant for Tommies. However the lady in charge received us very pleasantly, gave us quite a good tea, and at the end pressed upon us some cherries to eat on the journey. We went on to Rumpelmeyers again for another ice, picked up some parcels at the Westminster and drove to the Gare de Lyons. We dined in the station restaurant, a most lavishly decorated place up above the station, and looking down on to the platforms. We were in no great hurry as our places were all reserved. The train, described by the R.T.O. as the finest then running in Europe, was full to a seat, and we found ourselves all separated—in corridor carriages, three a side. With me I had three French officers, a French lady, and a Capt. Pilkington, Staff Captain on G.H.Q., Italy.

Saturday, 1st June.
We bowled along very fast and smoothly and as dawn broke came into some lovely country. We stopped at Chambery at 7.30 a.m. for an hour. We three got out and had breakfast at a little hotel opposite the station. I had some bread and butter and excellent chocolate. From there the mountains were finer every moment till we reached Modane on the frontier at midday. Here we stopped again for an hour and changed trains, having lunch meanwhile in the Hotel de l'Univers, just outside the station, and we began to hear Italian talked. There were one or two snow peaks visible from the village. From here we had Italian carriages, and an electric engine, and soon came to the M. Cenis tunnel, which we took twenty minutes to get through. We slid down the other side pretty quickly, the valley opening as we went and shewing some odd little villages perched up among the mountains, until we came to Turin at 5.30 p.m.—certainly a wonderful and magnificent journey. Here we fell into the arms of the R.T.O. and A.P.M., who were both most genial and kind and advised us to go to the Hotel Genoa. This we did, and the proprietor spoke English, which saved endless trouble. We each had a room, and after a wash and brush up went out to see the sights. The town is very handsome with broad clean paved streets and colonnades down each side of most of them, and trams everywhere. After dinner, at which we drank Asti Spumante, we saw three fine squares, one with a garden and fountain, and the third and largest three-sided, looking out on to the river, with green hills and cypresses beyond—most beautiful. We went into a sort of theatre in a big marquee for a short time, but could not understand a word said. Everything seems absurdly cheap here.

Sunday, 2nd June.
We paid our bill—66 lire for the three of us (about 35/-), including dinner, bed, and breakfast ; and then left by a passenger train at 10.30 a.m. for Arquata, the infantry base. We arrived at 3.30 p.m. after a very hot and airless journey, and were put up in a canvas camp, Wall and I sharing a tent. The camp is quite prettily situated in the Scrivia valley, and not so very far from Genoa. We went down into the village and dined at the Officers' Club, ran by Italian waiters, at which they gave us wild strawberries for dessert. It seems impossible that people should fight in such a country. There were some pleasant people from our camp, which comprises about twenty in all—one Boucher from the 1st Welch Fusiliers who is very particular about the Welch being spelt properly,

and Couchman from the 48th Bn. M.G.C. They have adopted the battalion system now instead of one company per brigade as in France before, which seems a pity. On the way back to camp we saw some fireflies, a novelty to me, but very uninteresting when caught.

Monday, 3rd June.

We had nothing official to do this morning and so Wall and I walked into the village and bought a Daily Mail. It is quite hot here, and some people wear pith helmets, though they all say it is the coolest place in Italy. We dined in camp this evening and went down to the Club afterwards. There was a gunner sub. there six foot eight inches high.

Tuesday, 4th June.

Heathcock was on a working party. Boucher, Wall and I walked into the next village away from Arquata and found it very hot. I saw the inside of my first Italian church, but it was all dismantled and soldiers were sleeping in it. We lunched at the Club. After tea I ran up a small hill behind the camp from which I got an excellent view, and did a small sketch, coming down in time for a jolly dinner at the Club. We were joined afterwards by the tall gunner and another sub. who, on the way back, insisted on stopping and shouting " corrections " at the flashes of summer lightning somewhere up in the Alps. We found ourselves detailed to our respective battalions. Heathcock and I are together, in the 48th, Wall goes elsewhere.

Wednesday, 5th June.

Spent the morning packing up, and lunched at the Club with Boucher and Couchman. Our train started at 1.40 p.m., and I had the misfortune to be saddled with the safe conduct of an officer under open arrest as far as his battalion in the line. The train at first was very full and we had to stand, but later on got seats with Heathcock and Wall. Arrived at Milan at 5 p.m. I took my charge off to the A.P.M. and found out that we could go straight on that night. The others were putting up at the Nord. After making these arrangements we joined up with them there and had tea and then went down to the Cathedral. This unfortunately was shut and so we had to be content with the outside : though that is marvellous enough. We dined all together in the arcade, a magnificent place, and went on to the opera, not in the Scala, which was closed, but in the Lyrico. We saw Lodoletta, conducted by the composer, Mascagni. I had to bring my fellow away before the last act in order to catch the midnight train.

Thursday, 6th June.

We changed at Vicenza in the small hours and reached Thiene at 8 a.m. This is railhead, just under the foot of the mountains. I was shaved in a barber's shop, and we breakfasted in the Officers' Club. We got a lorry about 11 a.m. and went up the mountain to Campiello, where we had to get out. It was a wonderful drive, zigzagging up the side all the time and giving the most splendid views southward towards Venice. We reached the battalion headquarters at last and I thankfully handed over my man, obtaining a written receipt for him. They gave me some tea, and then I caught a lorry back to Campiello, where I picked up the same man who

had driven me up in the morning. We flashed down pretty quickly and I got leave to put up in the Hotel Luna in Thiene. I had quite a respectable dinner there, with a dictionary in my hand, and went to the station to look for the others, but they didn't turn up.

Friday, 7th June.
Before breakfast I shaved off my moustache. At the club I saw the others, just come in by train. We said farewell to Wall, and then Heathcock, I, and three others managed to get a lorry up the hill once more. We reached the 48th Bn. M.G.C. at about 2 p.m. and reported to the Adjutant. The headquarters are perched up among the rocks just under the crest of a hill, so before tea we went up on to the top, all covered with fir trees, and quantities of beech fern and fragilis growing. We looked down upon the Austrian lines in the Asiago plateau, some six miles away, and I did a sketch. At tea we met Col. Clarke, C.M.G., D.S.O., &c., quite the commanding officer, but also very pleasant. He spoke to us afterwards and said something of the kind of life it was up here. We are about four thousand feet up, and he said one needs a lot to eat and shouldn't try to do too much at first, which seems most suitable. For quarters Heathcock and I shared the floor of a cubicle in a hut near by.

Saturday, 8th June.
Heathcock and I went out on to the hill behind before lunch. In the afternoon we were posted to companies, I alone to B, Heathcock to C. I went down to the company after tea with a runner, along a rocky path to some huts in a valley. It seemed quite extraordinary to be going at last as a machine gun officer into a company headquarters, and recalled very vividly some of the times I had had with the 183rd company before. I went into the mess, where I found Capt. Feild, the O.C., quite a good fellow; Webb, second in command, rather young; and two fellows from C company, Green and Heaphy, who have guns near. Feild went out after dinner and I slept on his bed, getting into pyjamas.

Sunday, 9th June.
At 11 a.m. I went out with Webb and sat on the forward slope of a hill, in full view, to watch an artillery strafe lasting half an hour. It seemed to me rather rash, but nothing came back. Then after tea I went up to section headquarters—No. 4 section, commanded by Lt. Hewson. He has a 2/Lt. Milner living with him, a red-headed fellow commanding No. 2 section. They are both pleasant, cheery, people. The headquarters is a small hut in a dell rather like a mine crater, with ferns and grass growing up the sides. There are two real spring beds in it. This is a good deal lower than battalion headquarters and not so far from the plateau. The two front lines are on opposite sides of a deep ravine, and beyond is a line of towering mountains clothed with pine woods to their tops.

Hewson said I could sleep, but I thought I would begin at once, and went round the guns with him at 10 p.m. Two of them were doing I.F. harassing fire, and I had my eyes opened a bit as to methods of laying guns in the line, as compared with Grantham. The maps, they say, are poor and not to be trusted for contours, but in many cases they lay direct, and check by the clinometer afterwards.

Monday, 10th June.

We went out again at 3.30 a.m. for stand to, and then turned in again for breakfast at 5 a.m., afterwards sleeping till midday. Two of the guns close here are in some curiously formed rocks, rather like pictures of the Dolomites. And the names on the map are so delightful—the house just above section headquarters is Brunialti, while not far away are Cunico, Stella, Canove, Tescia, Partut, and many others as charming. The day was gorgeous, with splendid visibility. The artillery did quite a big shoot from 11 to 3 p.m., but nothing came back. We went out again at 'stand to,' about 9.30 p.m., and wandered round till 11 p.m.

Tuesday, 11th June.

Up for stand to at 3.30 a.m. It began to rain about 4 a.m. and continued all day. There was another three-hour artillery strafe to-day. We went out again as usual at 9 p.m.; it was as black as pitch and rather slippery.

Wednesday, 12th June.

Rain still pouring down with no sign of its stopping. Out at the usual times. We do our harassing fire each night, generally on Ambrosini or Stella. There was no artillery strafe to-day: perhaps they couldn't see.

Thursday, 13th June.

A fine day again. The rain stopped while we were going round at stand to. After tea Hewson went back to battalion, as he is really signals officer, and is wanted for some job. Milner has shifted his headquarters, so I am left alone now, which is a little alarming. I wonder if the men realise the extent of my inexperience. I went round as usual, taking Sgt. Newman, the section sergeant, with me.

Friday, 14th June.

The night passed off quite well and without incident. The day was fine and hot, and I did not go out much. I went down to see the infantry battalions, and as they were sending out patrols I found I could not shoot till 3 a.m., which was rather late, so I sent up to Feild to ask if I should carry on, and he said I must.

Saturday, 15th June.

Just as I was getting up at 3 a.m. to go round the guns the Bosch started up with a big bombardment. Sgt. Newman and I raced round the two right hand guns. They had both gone back to their emplacements and were quite all right. All my guns were a good eight hundred yards behind the front line, so fortunately there was no danger of their being rushed. On crossing the small valley to the left pair of guns in their new positions we found it full of gas, tear gas mostly, but enough to make us put on our masks, and that made climbing up the steep sides of the valleys a most heart-breaking process. I continued to wander between the guns till about 6.30 a.m., when the shelling seemed to die down a bit, and Sgt. Newman and I had some breakfast together in the section headquarters. Then we went up to the Brunialti guns and stayed there till about 9 a.m., when Feild came round and said Newman had better go over to the left hand pair. By this time the Bosch had come

over—reaching our line at about 7.30 or 8.0 a.m. He pushed straight through all along except on the extreme left, and got on top of the Perghele ridge, about 600 yards in front of us, where we could see one of our Lewis gun teams. He came up farthest in the wood on our right, and by midday was level with us at Casa del Guardiano. I saw several Austrians standing inside the edge of the wood, about two hundred yards away, and had shots at them with a rifle.

For a time the situation seemed rather unpleasant, as we were expecting the Austrian to come round behind us any moment. Then our own infantry came up to man the Cesuna switch, where my guns were. I heard afterwards there were some 18-pounders firing into the wood over open sights, with some of our own guns supporting them, and this prevented the Austrian coming out. I stayed with the Brunialti guns all the time as there didn't seem to be much else to do. It was no good wandering to and fro between the two pairs of guns as I should have certainly been at the wrong place if anything had happened. As a matter of fact the Austrians did try to creep through the wire towards Cpl. Taylor's gun on the right, but half a belt settled their enterprise. On the left he tried to come down a trench on the near side of the Perghele ridge and was met by both my left hand guns and two others from another section, besides several Lewis guns. Our infantry tried two small counter attacks down through the wood at 5.30 p.m. and midnight, but were not successful. I stayed in the trench all the time with the right guns except to make one journey over to the others. During the afternoon the shelling had died down considerably, chiefly, I suppose, because the Austrian gunners didn't know where their own infantry were, which is hardly surprising considering the country. Towards evening he livened up a bit and appeared to register on our trench with a couple of shells, one within about five yards of the gun I was at. A comparatively small shell, bursting on bare rock, has quite a tremendous effect.

Sunday, 16th June.
We all expected he would attack again at dawn, and through the night the infantry raked the wood with Lewis guns and rifle fire. The Bosch remained quiescent until 3 a.m., when he opened up a Very light strafe of the largest description, sending up showers of lights of every imaginable colour and getting but the smallest response from his own guns and quite a lot from ours. Whether it was bluff or ' wind up ' no one seems to know, but nothing came of it, and in a couple of hours everything was quiet again. Then at 6.30 a.m. our own infantry did a silent counter attack through the wood—so quietly in fact that we didn't know of it until they had been in half an hour—and swept the board, completely clearing the wood and driving the Austrian back to his line—a really good performance, especially considering the ground they had to go over. Everything was so quiet that at 10 a.m. I left my guns and went over to see Fricker, commanding the section on my right, and went down into the wood with him. We found it full of Austrian bombs and rifles, and a good many Austrians there as well. They had evidently come to stay, judging by the quantity of stuff they had brought with them of all kinds. We found one fellow alive in a shelter with a badly-broken leg in a splint, and

brought some stretcher bearers up to him. He had some whiskey from Fricker's flask and asked for water, but we had none to give him. I asked him in German how he was, which he seemed to understand, though I couldn't make anything out of his answer. I picked up some souvenirs —two books, one in German, on physical training, and the other in some very strange tongue, a Czech dialect, I should think; and besides these a water bottle and two Very lights. After that I went back to section headquarters and slept for a while. In the afternoon I had a note down to say we should be relieved in the evening and so made preparations. Couchman of C company came down about 9.30 p.m. in pouring rain and took over. I showed him the two near guns and then went off with the runner as he knew the sector better than I did. I called in at Cesuna tunnel on the way back and saw Feild and Hewson for a moment, and then went on to Magna Boschi, where the men had some hot food. From there I took the men up a terrific hill to their positions in the Red line, which they had been to before, and so everything was quite simple.

Monday, 17th June.
I settled myself in at company headquarters at about 3.30 a.m. and slept till about 8 a.m. It began raining again in the afternoon. Feild came down and took me off with him to Area 6, on the "marginal road," running along on the extreme back edge of the hills; however when I got there I found it already crammed full with people, and so returned to Magna Boschi. The headquarters is in the possession of C company now. Capt. Wright is there, a somewhat erratic mad Irishman, Heaphy, whom I saw before, and one other.

Tuesday, 18th June.
Nothing of any interest. I went round my guns in the morning and had a good bath in the evening.

Wednesday, 19th June.
We got up for one of our own artillery shoots at 4 a.m., expecting the Bosche to reply, in which case we should retire up the rocks. However nothing happened and we came down again and had breakfast. Then I went up to my guns, which are mostly in "well" emplacements, like one near forward company headquarters at St. Quentin, blasted out of the solid rock. The position is magnificent, commanding the whole Astico valley and the mountains beyond. I did a sketch there.

Thursday, 20th June.
My section, and Milner's, who has been here with me, were relieved at midday. I went up to look round in the morning and then left my section to themselves, as I had to go to battalion headquarters to meet Feild, to bring up two of my corporals before the Colonel, because, unknown to me, they had dismounted their guns on the morning of the 15th, and had been found by some infantry in their dugout. After that we went on to Area 6 and there I and Milner both got beds, though the place is still pretty crowded. We put on pyjamas, which was a comfort, though we kept our ears on the stretch pretty well, expecting the Hun to attack in the morning or during the night.

Friday, 21st June.

Nothing happened this morning to our great relief, especially Milner's, who hopes to go on leave in two days' time. The clouds lifted to-day, and we had a glorious view out over the plain, with the Astico winding about for miles, almost down to Venice. I spent most of the day with the section cleaning up, &c.

Saturday, 22nd June.

There was a bit of a bombardment at midnight which occasioned some alarm, but otherwise all was well. Another fine day : Milner succeeded in getting off on leave. A company of the 7th Division came up to relieve us a day early, so we both have to squeeze into the accommodation for one. They seem a nice lot, and among them is Hamilton, one of my draft.

Sunday, 23rd June.

We spent the morning packing up. There was a thick cloud down on the mountain preventing us from seeing anything. At 2 o'clock I took 2 and 4 sections by the mule track down the hill, across the Astico and up the other side on to a foothill to a place called Rua. It was a splendid walk down, and I saw a wonderful lot of flowers by the way. We all crept into little Italian bivouac tents in the orchard of a farm where we mess. The house is very large, with windows dotted about it promiscuously. Two different families at least seem to live in it, and a swarm of animals in or near. There are vines round, and a few walnut and fig trees.

Monday, 24th June.

It is hot down here, though we are about a thousand feet above sea level. Nothing much to do in the morning except clean up. After lunch Feild took Hewson and myself to look at a range near by where we shall fire.

Tuesday, 25th June.

We paraded in the morning. In the afternoon there was a scare that we should have to go up the line again, as they thought the Austrian was going to have another try. Fortunately nothing came of it. Children come round here selling oranges, which are rather good, and we eat them a good deal.

Wednesday, 26th June.

C company and battalion came down this evening and we gave them dinner. C company and ourselves mess in the same large room of this farm. I saw Heathcock, who seems to be enjoying life.

Thursday, 27th June—Sunday, 30th June.

We paraded in the mornings from 9-1 and generally had the afternoons off. Friday it rained hard all day and nearly washed us away—a passing storm, as Saturday was as fine and hot as could be. Boucher, of the 1st Welch Fusiliers, came over and dined with us one day. Sunday there was a church parade and a Celebration.

Monday, 1st July.

We spent the day cleaning and packing up. I have No. 2 section now to look after—really Milner's, but he is on leave still. At 8 p.m. we started off and marched down the hill to Thiene and passed through without a stop. Just beyond there they produced a horse, which I was obliged to ride for a while, though I got off after about an hour and a half. We passed Malo about midnight and went on over the hills to Priabona and finally Tezze, which we reached in daylight.

Tuesday, 2nd July.

The last part was rather trying as we all thought the place to be nearer than it really was, and an extra mile at the end of twenty is rather hard to manage. However marching by night in the cool was infinitely preferable to going by day. We reached Tezze at about 6 a.m. The men have an excellent billet, and we quite a good mess, but poor bedroom, shared between four—Hewson, Webb, Stafford, and myself. However we got into our beds and slept till midday. The afternoon was spent in unpacking limbers under the eye of the C.O., who made himself rather annoying.

Wednesday, 3rd July,

Was a day off, in which we did nothing but check gun stuff.

Thursday, 4th July.

We spent the morning, 7-1, on the range. I marched the company out. On the way a car passed and stopped and out got Morshead, who walked with me for about a mile and a half talking very pleasantly. In appearance he is quite unchanged, though his manner is that of the complete staff officer, with spurs. He is G.S.O. 2, 48th Division, now. The range, when we reached it, consisted of a little valley with the targets half way up one steep side, and the guns on a path along the other face. There is a cottage or two quite close, but they are so far undamaged. I fired myself a little—not so badly. The afternoons are tremendously hot, and one can't do much. After dinner I went down to the river and had quite a nice bathe. The water is quite warm and not much above five feet deep anywhere.

Friday, 5th July.

I was orderly dog, which entailed a good deal of guard mounting and dismounting, &c., &c., conducted by a spruce sergeant-major, who reminds me rather of the 'Red Queen.' I had to go on the usual company parades as well. In addition to this, however, I managed to find a billet for myself in a house not too far away, which is much better than being cooped up with the others. I have a double bed and sheets. I also acquired a permanent servant, by name Wigley, who seems very good, and has done the job before. My first servant, Price, was removed to hospital. Milner said I killed him, making him carry my valise from the Brunialti headquarters to the Cesuna road. But he was found lying in a field near Thiene sniping with a rifle at passers by on the main road!

1918

Saturday, 6th July—Tuesday, 9th July.

Spent a good deal of time on the range practising for a firing competition which is to come off on the 10th, to decide the best sub-section in the battalion. The firing is at small iron plates on the range, 300 yards across the valley. The men are very keen, and so am I. We parade too long, and too much in the heat of the day, which is a pity, and is knocking up some of the men.

Wednesday, 10th July.

I out on the range by 8 a.m. to judge for C company's firing in the competition. Some of their teams are quite good. B company came on at 2 p.m. Hamilton and Biddick, my two star teams, were knocked out by No. 4 section, though I was rather doubtful about the scoring, however! Warner and Crisp did splendidly, getting 47 out of 50 their first shoot. In the final they were beaten by No. 3 section, which was rather disappointing. It was very hot all day. We rather surprised the weak minds of some of the other company officers there by the speed with which the B company teams came into action. Fifteen seconds is not so bad.

Thursday, 11th July.

Spent a very boring, not to say annoying, morning doing pack transport with mules.

Friday, 12th July—Wednesday, 17th July.

Paraded once in the dry river bed, bombing, and on the 30-yard range. The final of the shooting was on Saturday, when No. 3 section lost to C company. The whole time it was shockingly hot, and on Monday, after eating some meat, my inside gave up the struggle. I dieted myself on eggs and neat tea after fasting as long as I could stand it.

Thursday, 18th July.

After resting all day I left on a lorry at 4 p.m. and went to Sarcedo camp at Ca Paiella, just outside Thiene. Here I saw Heathcock, and No. 2 section, who had come on ahead.

Friday, 19th July.

I saw the battalion off at 4.30 a.m. and met the company, going out on a bicycle and guided them into the camp. Here we spent the day, sweltering under the trees. The tents were much too hot to go in. I saw some curious little lizards running about on the stone walls.

Saturday, 20th July.

This was about the worst day of all, for heat and everything.

Sunday, 21st July.

The company went off at 4.0 a.m. I went on a lorry, as being more or less incapable, to Mare, on the foot hills, about a thousand feet up. I had a tent and went to bed on arrival. It was a good deal cooler there, and there were plenty of shady trees.

Monday, 22nd July.
   Stayed in bed again, feeling rather better. We had a thorough big thunderstorm in the evening with torrents of rain, which cooled things down a bit.

Tuesday, 23rd July.
   The company moved at 4 a.m. to march up the hills to Granezza. I went on a lorry at 6 a.m. and had the most marvellous drive up the hills, with the sun just risen, making the colouring glorious : one of the finest drives I have ever gone. We went up to the right of our old sector getting in at 7.30 a.m. The company arrived at 8 a.m. Our quarters are in a wooden hut made by the Italians rather like a Swiss châlet, with separate little bedrooms for each of us. I saw the doctor to-day, went to bed at 11 a.m., and stayed there all day.

Wednesday, 24th July—Friday, 26th July.
   I stayed in bed till tea time on Wednesday and felt better for it. The air is much nicer up here, and it never gets really hot. The other days were spent generally in preparing for the line.

Saturday, 27th July.
   Up to the line. Actually down hill for a couple of miles towards the Asiago plateau and then to the left, a scrambling path among the rocks to the company headquarters. I am with Feild this time, acting as second in command, as Webb is away. Feild was out all the afternoon, but came back in time for dinner, and stayed in all night. The dugout is small, and built of logs, and quite comfortable.

Sunday, 28th July.
   Feild out again all the morning. I went round the sections at 2 p.m., quite a long walk, and met rations on the main road at 6. There who should I see but A. H. Press of the old 183rd company come to join this company as a reinforcement. Very odd, and very pleasant. He came up to headquarters and stayed the night with us.

Monday, 29th July.
   I took Press round to No. 4 section in the morning and also saw Milner, behind the S. Sisto ridge, who is rather bad with my complaint, and Stafford, in front. I got back for lunch and stayed in the rest of the day. After going round the guns in this sector one does not want to do very much more—there is so much up and down steep hills. From the top of the hill in front of headquarters to the front line is a drop of about 600 feet in little over a mile. The whole sector is covered with trees, except for one big clearing from which you get an excellent view of Asiago, and the plateau generally. Feild told me I am being sent off for a rest to-morrow to Lake Garda.

Tuesday, 30th July.
   I off to battalion in the morning and lunched there. Then on to Fara by lorry, down a different road from that by which I came up. I had tea

at transport lines, or B echelon, as they prefer to call it, and then went on by lorry again to Thiene. I put up at the Club and dined at the Luna, where in a rash moment I had some chicken, which I was sorry for afterwards.

Wednesday, 31st July.
I joined a crowd of officers and men at the station in time for the 5 a.m. train and formed a party with two officers from the 4th Gloucesters —Stone and Dutton—also going to Garda. We went down by Vicenza to Peschiere, where we got on board a boat and steamed across a corner of the lake to Sirmione. We were in all about 50 officers and 300 men, I should think. We live in the Grand Hotel, Regie Terme; two officers to a bedroom, and meals at small tables in the hotel dining-room. Everything seems to be very well done, and there is no official nonsense about it. I walked out in the afternoon and sat down near the end of the peninsula on the cliff looking at the lake, which at times is almost as blue as the Blauzee above Interlaken. We had an excellent dinner, including whitebait and a cream ice, at which I was entirely reckless.

Thursday, 1st August.
Rather a poor night. I find the heat rather in the way here. However heat or no I went in a motor launch over to Gardone with the two Gloucesters. There was not much to do there. The place consists almost entirely of large hotels, all of which were shut up. We took our lunch and ate it on the boat. On the way back we circled round the Ile de Garda, a most fairy-like place, then over almost to the east side of the lake, and so back by tea time.

Friday, 2nd August—Sunday, 4th August.
The first two days I spent mostly on my bed reading. My meal companions—Stone and Dutton—are very pleasant people. We have a table to ourselves now near a French window.
Sunday afternoon there was a bit of a storm and I went to my perch on the cliff at the end of the " almost island " and watched the waves and tried to sketch in my field notebook. After dinner a man came in and played rather well on a piano, chiefly Liszt and Chopin.

Monday, 5th August.
We three went in a small steamer to Salo. Again the place seemed mostly shut up, though we managed to have lunch in a small hotel, and wandered about the town, or village it really is. I bought one of d'Annunzio's novels in Italian to try and read.

Tuesday, 6th August.
I stayed in until lunch time and read ' Horace Blake ' by Mrs. Wilfrid Ward, borrowed from the canteen library. After tea I went down with Stone and bathed. The water was warm and amazingly clear. I also did a sketch or rather copied a rather strangely carved stone set in the wall of the street under an archway.

GRANEZZA—S. SISTO

Wednesday, 7th August.

Our last day, and it has been such a delightful time, so different from anything else I ever did in the Army. Our doctor came in with the new arrivals. We left at 3 p.m. by steamer as before, waited some time for the train at Peschiere, and changed at Vicenza, reaching Thiene by 10 p.m., where I succeeded in losing my waterproof ground sheet. I saw Col. Clarke for a moment in the Club, just going on leave, and then went across to the Luna to my bedroom.

Thursday, 8th August.

Breakfast comfortably at the Luna. I caught a lorry at the door of the Officers' Club, which took me up to Carriola, where I made enquiries for my ground sheet, and then another lorry along the marginal road past 'Area 6' to Granezza. I had lunch at battalion, where I reported, and then went down to the company, now out of the line. They are doing a barrage to-night for a big raid, so I went up with Milner to the clearing and helped him lay eight guns. As I was not wanted to fire I came away, getting back by 11.30 p.m. The show began at midnight and made a great noise.

Friday, 9th August.

A good raid apparently. Rested most of the day. I have my own little cubicle again to sleep in. Another bombardment to-night, as the French are repeating last night's performance, on our right.

Saturday, 10th August.

We had boxing this morning instead of P.T. Hamilton and Webb put up quite a spirited show. Major Baron and two others came to dine. During dinner the men boxed in a ring put up near our mess, and later, to everyone's intense joy, a couple of Italians came down and were persuaded to join in. One of them had such long hair that he had to stop constantly and shake it out of his eyes. Altogether a most entertaining evening.

Sunday, 11th August.

A very hot and tedious church parade in the cinema, followed by Communion, to which I went. Spent the afternoon reading.

Monday, 12th August.

No. 2 section on fatigue round the transport lines. I had to leave them to-day in favour of Milner, to whom they really belong. I am sorry, but it is only fair. I take over No. 4, the one I had first at Cesuna; not such a good lot, I think. Bright, of the 144th Brigade L.T.M.'s, came in to dine.

Tuesday, 13th August—Thursday, 15th August.

Nothing special : ordinary training and fatigues.

Friday, 16th August.

I left at 3 a.m. with Milner and our two sections to go up the line. We had a long walk down the road, turning off behind the S. Sisto ridge. I am left forward section, he is right forward. We each have a couple of guns in front of the wire which cannot be reached in daylight. My section

headquarters is quite a good place and very safe—about 20 feet of rock on top. I share it with my servant and three signallers, who seem quite a nice lot. We had a bit of shelling from 11.30 to 1.0 p.m., but nothing else of particular interest. At 9.0 p.m. I went out to R. 3 and 4 in front of the wire to spend the night.

Saturday, 17th August.
A quiet night. The Austrian sends up a good many lights, which is always a good sign. I came back to section headquarters at 5.30 a.m. and spent the morning checking the position of R. 7 and 8 by the compass. In the afternoon I went over to see Milner, going along the front line, which has been blasted out of the solid rock nearly all the way. From him I went to Read (No. 1 section) behind the S. Sisto ridge, and on to the 4th Gloucesters' headquarters, where I saw Stone and Dutton, who gave me tea. Feild and Webb turned up while I was there. Out again at 9 p.m.

Sunday, 18th August.
Gentle night. The moon is getting nearly full, and so the number of lights diminishes a good deal. He is fond of sending up red and green lights without any artillery response at all. One wonders rather why he does it. I slept till lunch time, when I had a grand spread with wild strawberries and whortleberries which Wigley picked. Milner came in to tea and had some, and Blackmore (No. 3 section) looked in afterwards.

Monday, 19th August.
Very fine night and very few lights until, soon after midnight, there was some excitement near Canove leading to a large display of Very lights, white, green, and orange, but no artillery. We turn on a searchlight every now and then to Catz and Rodighieri, and places behind the line. The Austrian uses one too, sometimes. The early mornings are perfectly lovely for the colours, as the light touches first the tops of the hills and then creeps down into the valley, though the Ghelpac always seems dark and sinister. I took some more bearings in the morning and Milner came in to lunch. Really Wigley quite surpassed himself. I had eggs, as I am still off meat : Milner had a rissole and two vegetables. Then we went on to biscuit pudding, followed by dessert of three fruits, and custard; the fruit all " off the estate." Not so bad for the line. We agreed that these " liaison lunches," as we called them, must be repeated. I slept most of the afternoon, and Blackmore came in to tea. I spend my spare time reading the books the signallers get from the Y.M.C.A. library at Granezza.

Tuesday, 20th August.
Splendid night and full moon : no lights till 3.0 a.m. Slight disturbance at midnight opposite us, and some M.G. bullets came over the position, but nothing more. Our guns did a " destructive shoot " on the left of Asiago—the Edelweiss spur—from 7.30 to 11.30 a.m. and made a lot of noise. Quiet afternoon. I had tea with Blackmore and saw Milner. The Austrian did a bit of a shoot from 5.30 to 7.0 p.m., but nothing very much.

Wednesday, 21st August.

Another good night, with a bit of an infantry show at midnight. I went over at the morning ' stand to ' in front of the wire to see Milner's forward guns, and saw Cpl. Hamilton and No. 7 team. Quite a hot day. I slept till lunch as usual.

Thursday, 22nd August.

Fine night. Not out much during the day.

Friday, 23rd August.

I fired with three guns from 3.30 a.m. till dawn, at some wire—ranges varying from 2,500 to 2,850 yards, which last was too short. Webb ironically sent down some anti-aircraft precautions for high angle fire. Milner came in after lunch and I went round to the infantry companies. Orders came down for a relief to-morrow. These were cancelled at 11.15 p.m., most annoying.

Saturday, 24th August.

Rather disturbed night : people firing rifles and throwing bombs, &c. all the time. Nothing much to do until the evening, when I changed over with Press and No. 3 section. This relief was considerably accelerated on hearing of an infantry raid timed for 10.0 p.m. I put most of the men in dugouts under the S. Sisto ridge, and sheltered there myself with Milner who had also come back. There was a good deal of stuff back, including one direct hit on the S. Sisto dressing station ; but as there is three feet of concrete on the top nothing was damaged.

Sunday, 25th August.

My new section headquarters, in among the trees behind the left hand end of the S. Sisto ridge, is quite a good place with a strong roof of logs. I have Wigley in to sleep there with me as there are two beds, but not really room for two to live permanently. We did a bombardment from 8.15 to 11.0 a.m. I did some Morse code, in which I have become rather interested, since living with the signallers at the forward section H.Q.

Monday, 26th August.

Not very well this morning, perhaps as a result of the local dessert of raspberries and whortleberries : so I spent most of the day on my bed. Another big raid this evening. We sheltered again under the ridge and I met Walford, late of the 2/8th Worcs., now with the 1st 8th.

Tuesday, 27th August.

The show finished by 1.30 a.m., and we went back to our beds. I spent most of the day again on mine and practised Morse.

Wednesday, 28th August.

Rather better. I went up the clearing at ' stand to ' and had a glorious view over the plateau. Each little fold in the ground has its cloud of mist, and everything is the most delicate colour imaginable. I then went back to my bed till lunch, which I had with Milner, very enjoyably : then back to my bed again. Feild came down after tea. After he had gone

the Hun put over three 11-inch shells, one of which landed only about an hundred yards away, uprooting about a dozen trees and throwing rocks about all over the place. I looked at the hole afterwards, which is about twenty feet deep : not at all nice.

Thursday, 29th August.
We were relieved in the morning by A company. I walked out after the men had gone, with Tustin, my runner. The Admiral of the 144th T.M. Battery gave me some tea at their headquarters on the road, which I was very glad of, having had no breakfast before starting. I reached the billets about 11.30 a.m., and then came inspections of gun kit, clothes, &c., &c., lasting into the afternoon. At 7 p.m. I had to take my section up to the anti-aircraft positions behind and above Division. As it happened there was a thunderstorm going on at the time, and so we all got properly soaked through. The positions are in part of the " marginal line " or last line of defence before the edge of the hills. Luckily the mules just managed to carry the guns up. There are two guns each side of the valley, some six or seven hundred yards apart. Accommodation this side was scanty, consisting of a large dugout blasted out of the solid rock, which dripped faster than the rain—the men went into this—and some gun emplacements, too low to stand upright and too small to lie straight—I went into one of these. The main advantage of the position is its inaccessibility. People do not care to take the trouble to climb up and see what one is doing.

Friday, 30th August.
I woke up about 8.30 a.m. to a gorgeous morning. In the distance, well into Austria, I could see one or two mountains covered with snow : one being, I think, the Cima d'Asta, about 8,800 feet, behind the Brenta : altogether a splendid view. The men do a good deal of signalling here to the other pair of guns, mostly semaphore, which they know best. I am trying to teach them Morse. Though apparently so close it takes half an hour to get from one pair to the other, each side entailing a climb of two or three hundred feet. I tried morsing with my electric torch when it grew dark, but I sha'n't do that any more as it is so bright a light.

Saturday, 31st August—Sunday, 1st September.
Nothing much to do. Practised signalling mostly. I feel much better up here, and had some grapes which Wigley bought for me down below at a lira and a half for three bunches.

Monday, 2nd September.
A bad day. Rain began in the night and clouds stayed low on the hills almost all day. I had my relief orders in the morning, and just managed, in an interval, to signal them over to the other side by semaphore. Press came up and relieved me at 6 p.m., and I went down and slept in pyjamas very comfortably. Before going to bed, however, I was told I had to go down the hills to the 7th Divisional sports in the morning, with Feild and some others, though I would much rather have stayed behind and rested.

Tuesday, 3rd September.
Up at 7.30 a.m. and to Granezza, where we got into lorries to go to this show. Besides Feild there was Major Baron, Lt. Couchman, whom I met at Arquata, and one or two more. We had a splendid drive down the hills and through Thiene to Trissino, which is just short of Tezze. The sports, in a huge meadow, were very well arranged indeed, and everything very nice. I saw a good many people I knew, one or two Marlburians, Calderari, now an interpreter, Morshead, and Lomax, a regular and quite the Lt.-Col., commanding the 21st Manchesters: Brooks, who was with me at Lloyd's, Hartley Wintney, now a Bde. Major, and one or two more. There was some very fine horse jumping, which roused even my admiration, and several other amusing events. In fact quite a good show. We left at 7.30 p.m. and dined in Thiene on the way back at 9. Then on up the hill, passing, on the way, a couple of huge tractors drawing some of the spare parts of an Italian 12-inch gun. Bed at 12.30 a.m.

Wednesday, 4th September—Thursday, 5th September.
My camp bed, which I sent for some time ago, has now come, and is pleasanter to sleep on than the stretched sandbags we get here. Nothing of interest beyond a hair cut and bath.

Friday, 6th September.
Forward again with Milner at 3 a.m. There was a raid by the French at 5 a.m., and in response to that we had some shells near us: afterwards it was pretty quiet. I am in the same dugout with the signals. In the evening, after I had gone out to R. 3 and 4, the Italians blasted the S. Sisto road, making it wider, with 64 explosions. I don't know what the Austrians must have thought. They did not take much notice at the time, though at 10.15 p.m. and again at 12.15 a.m., he shelled the front line and the gap behind us quite briskly for a few minutes each time.

Saturday, 7th September—Sunday, 8th September.
Nothing of interest. I read the Loom of Youth, brought down by the signallers: a bad book.

Monday, 9th September.
Quiet day. There were two raids during the night for which I cleared R. 3 and 4 as much as possible and went with the men to a dugout in the front line, according to Feild's orders. There was quite a lot of shelling for the first one, but for the second he seemed to have used up most of his ammunition, and also his white Very lights, having to be content for the rest of the night with red and green.

Tuesday, 10th September.
Our cookhouse was knocked in last night by a 4.2. Quite a good day. Press relieved me after dark, and I went back to the support section positions.

Wednesday, 11th September.
I went up the clearing in the morning to R. 16 and on to company headquarters, where I saw Feild and Webb. I stayed there till about 11.30 a.m. and had some cocoa, coming down with Feild to R. 15 and my

other positions. We are making a new dugout close to section headquarters for the men with a roof of " my own invention," something on the lines of Victoria station. Feild laughs, but I think it will be fairly strong and dry.

Thursday, 12th September.
Splendid sleep last night, which I continued till lunch time, after going up the clearing at stand to. The full score of the 'Mass in D' came, which I had asked for, and is absorbingly interesting.

Friday, 13th September.
Up the clearing at stand to : glorious sunrise and colouring over the plateau. Feild came up in the morning and brought Dixon, a new comer, to live with me, which is rather a bore. It will be rather a struggle fitting the two of us into this little place : however. Milner came over to lunch.

Saturday, 14th September.
Up the clearing again at sunrise, also at mid-day, and again at evening stand to. Pretty tired. We did a gas bombardment at 10 p.m., but had nothing back.

Sunday, 15th September.
I slept till lunch. Nice day. Visited Milner after tea, and then up the clearing at 8 p.m. to lay two guns for night firing. I saw the Oxford and Bucks about it, quite pleasant people, who gave me a whiskey and soda ! I fired from the middle of the clearing from 9 p.m. to 12.30 a.m., when we had to stop because of infantry patrols. It was very cold.

Monday, 16th September.
We were relieved early in the morning by A company. Immediately on getting out we had to parade for new eye-pieces to our box respirators, followed by a section kit inspection. After lunch I went down and had a bath, going on to C company for tea, where I saw Heathcock, who invited me to dine. I went down about 8 o'clock with Webb and had quite an amusing evening.

Tuesday, 17th September.
A good long night. In the morning the company was inspected by Major Long. After lunch I went off to reconnoitre some gun positions near the Kaberlaba road, which I occupy in case of a strafe, though I doubt if we should ever get there. After that all the officers had to go up to battalion headquarters for a harangue by the C.O., who told us all off like pickpockets.

Wednesday, 18th September.
On parade all the morning. About 11.30 p.m. an 11-inch shell came down just across the road and caused an immense sensation. In the afternoon we had a court-martial promulgation, and then later on a giving of medals—two Italian Croces de Guerra—by the G.O.C., Gen. Walker.

GRANEZZA

Thursday, 19th September.

Paraded all the morning. After lunch we all trooped up to battalion again, when Major Long gave us a lecture on the new Representation of the People Bill. After that Cpl. Hamilton, a first rate gunner and shining light in Milner's section, was had up to orderly room, severely reprimanded, and told to take his stripes down, for making a fool of himself at Sirmione. I call it very unjust. The doctor, Major Baron, and the senior Padre, one Crawley, M.C. bar, came to dine.

Friday, 20th September.

Nothing much to do. Webb and I dined with D company, where were Baron, Fricker, and Sproule. Cpl. Hamilton goes to them to-morrow, so I put a word in beforehand.

Saturday, 21st September.

In the afternoon B and D companies played football. I went up and watched with Milner. Afterwards we went to the cinema at the Curios, and saw a Chaplin film.

Sunday, 22nd September.

No parades all day : an excellent scheme. Breakfast 9.15 a.m., then a voluntary church service and Communion at 11.30. After lunch I went a walk to the marginal road and sat for some time looking over to the plains. We went to the cinema again at 8 and saw some fresh pictures.

Monday, 23rd September.

Parades more or less all day, packing up for the line.

Tuesday, 24th September.

Relieved at 3.30 a.m. with Milner as usual, in pouring rain. I in the signals dugout as before.

Wednesday, 25th September.

Rain all night. Pretty beastly at R. 3 and 4. Spent some of the time mending the roof at R. 3 men's dugout. I stayed in most of the morning.

Thursday, 26th September.

Nice night. Put out some 'tactical' wire with the help of a sapper, towards R. 2, and saw Milner engaged on the same job. During the afternoon I made an expedition along the front line to the next company front, and saw Hamilton, in charge of a gun.

Friday, 27th September—Wednesday, 2nd October.

Up the line all the time, and the usual routine. I had one liaison lunch with Milner.

Thursday, 3rd October.

We were relieved by A company. I went back with Milner via company headquarters and there heard I should have to come up again and fire the barrage for a raid. I had a bath, and then at 5.30 p.m. Milner and I went up in a lorry with Feild and laid the guns in daylight in the clearing.

After that I arranged myself in a dugout in the wood with my two teams. There was a smoky brazier, and so I had to lie on the floor to avoid choking, but all the same I had a most amusing time listening to the men talking. Among other gems was a story of Pte. Appleby, one of the less intellectually distinguished of my section. Asked by an officer " Where's Sec ? " —Sec being a house in the Austrian lines and a very well known landmark —he is reported to have answered, " I don't know, sir, he's not on my team."

Friday, 4th October.
At 4.30 a.m. I fired the barrage for the raid, continuing till 5.40 a.m. We had quite a good time and had nothing back. After that we went back quite easily and quietly. Nothing to do during the day, except clean guns.

Saturday, 5th October.
Parades all day. In the afternoon the C.O. came along and inspected the company, presenting a flag to us, with a speech.

Sunday, 6th October.
Nice day. No church. Went a walk with Blackmore to the marginal line and to see Milner on the way back at the A.A. positions. Blackmore and I both expected to fire a barrage for a French raid, but instead I was sent up to relieve Milner and he had to go down and fire. I got up by 5 p.m. and settled in, in a hut this time, with an excellent canvas bed like a well. The French raid was off after all.

Monday, 7th October.
Lovely morning. Nothing much doing. Heard in the afternoon that I am to be temporarily second in command of D company, under Hugman, on account of some bétise of one of their people. I don't at all care about it. Press relieved me at 3 p.m., and I had tea with B company on the way down to D. I dined there and went to the Curios with Milner and Blackmore.

Tuesday, 8th October.
I took a bathing parade in the morning. Nothing else to do.

Wednesday, 9th October.
Snow in the morning : rain for the rest of the day. I went to B company in the afternoon and battalion in the evening.

Thursday, 10th October—Friday, 11th October.
Rain all the time. The second morning the French did their raid, B company firing for them. During the day there were four artillery strafes lasting an hour each, making a great noise. There is an Italian 11-inch howitzer within an hundred yards of this billet which lifts the roof and floor boards every time it fires. We had a rather interesting lecture by the senior Padre, with maps, on the war and Germany's aims, the Berlin-Baghdad railway, &c., &c. I bathed in the evening.

KABERLABA—ASIAGO

Saturday, 12th October.

D company into the line. I came up with Hugman in a lorry, a very gentlemanly way of going up, to left company headquarters : not at all a bad place—a collection of small huts in a valley, with crocuses growing in the grass outside the door. I saw Heathcock and Green in the evening as they were coming out.

Sunday, 13th October—Wednesday, 16th October.

Rain all the time. I did a certain amount of wandering about, going to the different guns in turn. This company sector is much more hilly and broken than ours.

Thursday, 17th October.

Fine day at last. Down to the left hand guns in the morning, and at dusk up to Kaberlaba, where, close to the houses, I got an excellent view of the surrounding country. One of the officers of my reinforcement draft is buried not far from our headquarters, killed on June 15th.

Friday, 18th October—Saturday, 19th October.

Rain again nearly all the time. Friday we heard that Lille and Ostend were taken.

Sunday, 20th October.

Relieved by C company : I out all the way on a lorry. I saw Major Baron and Fricker, now back from leave, and settled up with D company, going back to B company after dinner very gladly.

Monday, 21st October—Thursday, 24th October.

Milner, Blackmore and I went to the Curios twice and saw some pictures. Between times there were the usual parades. Wednesday night I took my section up to hold the line while A company fired a barrage for a raid. On the mountains opposite there is quite a lot of snow.

Friday, 25th October.

Had a rather interesting time on the range firing stoppages. We had the divisional band down in the afternoon, which played quite nicely.

Saturday, 26th October.

We spent the whole morning preparing for an inspection by the C.O. at 12.15 p.m., but he did not appear till 2.15 p.m. We stayed in in the evening.

Sunday, 27th October.

Up with Milner as usual at 4 a.m. for R. 3 and 4. I spent the day in the signal dugout.

Monday, 28th October.

Awfully cold night, and very long. 'Stand to' lasts from 6 p.m. to 6.30 a.m., so I have to have a 'high tea' instead of dinner before going out. Nothing much to do during the day.

Tuesday, 29th October.
The Warwicks raided in front of us at 2.15 a.m. No one was there except 'Very light Joe' and a friend, the former being killed and the other hit. The Bosch has apparently gone back to his winter line near the foot of the hills. In the afternoon I made a rather interesting expedition with Wigley and Horton, one of the signallers, out in front. We went to Nameless House and Sec, then on to point 1020 and back through Asiago. His front line has been fearfully battered about, hardly existing in some places.

Wednesday, 30th October.
Very cold at R. 3 and 4. The men make some tea about midnight and give me a share, which is 'grateful and comforting,' as is also the rum, which runs to about a spoonful a man twice a night. The day was beautifully clear.

Thursday, 31st October.
Nothing to do by day. We have a tiny brazier of charcoal now at R. 3, which makes things much pleasanter, though it gave me a terrific headache in the morning.

Friday, 1st November.
At 4.45 a.m. orders came round from Feild that the Division would attack at dawn! It was a terrific scramble. First I had to collect all four guns at R. 3 and 4, where I was, and then rush round to the back of the S. Sisto ridge and find the Berks, with whom I was to act. Finally, after a good deal of scurrying about, two mules came down and we loaded up with 15 and 16 teams stuff, L.-Cpl. Farmar and Cpl. Sherwood. The other two teams were to come on later. We left R. 3 and 4 at 6.30 a.m. in daylight, never to go back there. I reported to the Berks advanced headquarters in Asiago at a few minutes past seven, having come along the road through Ave. There was very little shelling indeed, though by this time the infantry attack must have been well started, but there were a few bursts of M.G. fire coming into the town as we came through. The old Major (Battcock) of the Berks was in a great state of excitement, fussing about in a cellar. Already there were some prisoners coming in, including a couple of officers. Presently the Brigadier came in and Feild, and he said I had better go and look for positions further forward. I went out, taking L.-Cpl. Noond and Pte. Tutchings, and moved forward in the direction of Rodighieri. About 600 yards short of this we had a pretty near go from some 5.9's, several of which dropped within about fifteen or twenty yards—quite unpleasant. Luckily the ground was very soft there, and so the shells went down a long way before exploding, making very large craters, but bursting entirely upwards, not outwards. After that we moved to the left and found some places which would do, and went back. I then brought up the two teams and we settled down in a small hollow just under the crest at half-past ten. Here we stayed for some hours and most of the men went to sleep. About 4 p.m. I made some cocoa with my tommy cooker. We had had no shells near us all the time, though some came over on our left, beyond Capitello Mulche.

At 5 p.m. I moved forward and put the guns in shell holes commanding the road junction south of Bosco, and the men in a house close by, which was rather warmer than being in the open. After we had settled in I rushed up M. Catz with Wigley to see the Berks again, which was a most exhausting process. I spent most of the night in the house with the men. The Bosch was evidently still on Camporovere spur, because when some one struck a match which showed through the window he loosed off a stream of M.G. bullets straight down the road past the house, and continued sniping at intervals most of the night.

Saturday, 2nd November.

At dawn I moved one gun forward into Bosco to cover a proposed infantry attack on a trench behind it. Everything seemed very quiet, however; and soon after my gun was in position we saw our own infantry walking about in the objective and on my target, so I dismounted the gun and sent back for the other one. This came up soon and we moved forward at 8.15 a.m., still with the two mules up the road leading over M. Mosciagh. It was hard going, as the road was steep, and we were all carrying fairly heavy loads, and so halted every quarter of an hour. At a quarter past ten I met Milner at a place where there was a battery of 4.2's all in position. We arrived at the top a bit later, the mules doing some marvellous climbing on the way, and I joined on to Milner, who was with the Bucks. We expected to stay there and billeted the men in sheds near by. There was a 5.9 battery at the top, and one or two of the men got most excellent clinometers. Soon after we had come there Feild arrived and I went with him to souvenir an artillery division headquarters. I found a really splendid periscope which I carried away. We also souvenired a typewriter which we hid in a blanket for future use. Milner presented me with a pair of fur-lined Austrian gloves tied together with a string, like trench gloves. The men found a bag of potatoes, and began making a stew. Our last discovery was a whole box full of medals, complete with ribbons: every man in Milner's and my section had one! Then suddenly we had orders to move down into the Valle Portule. Rather than abandon their stew two men carried it on a pole between them. We arrived at the bottom of the valley about 5 p.m., having acquired a small handcart on the way, which was quite useful. We were billeted in a hut close to brigade. Feild, Milner, Press and I, and the O.C. 145th T.M.'s were all in a little room with four beds, of which I had one. Sgt. Newman and the other two teams joined up with us here. I gave my periscope to Sgt. Naish to take back for me safely out of the way.

Sunday, 3rd November.

We moved at 4.15 a.m., in pitch dark, down into the Val d'Assa, with the Berks again this time, my whole section together, and five mules. It was a considerable struggle getting off, and still more so moving up the Val d'Assa as the men were pretty tired. We had to abandon the handcart before very long. However we were cheered first by the dawn, then by the sight of large batches of prisoners coming back, and a little later by seeing several cars pass with Austrian and English officers, bearing

large white flags. This extraordinary sight helped us along in a most marked way. At about ten o'clock we crossed the Austrian frontier, as I could see from my map, and a few minutes later a message was passed down by the men from the head of the column to say we were in Austria. We halted for three quarters of an hour on the top, by Vessena, and there I had some cocoa and the men made tea, with Austrian sugar, of which they found a great lump as big as one's head.

About 1 p.m. we passed a huge prisoners' camp of Austrians. All along the road were blankets, water bottles, and kit of various kinds, to say nothing of rifles and even machine guns left lying; obvious signs of a very precipitate retreat.

While climbing up M. Mosciagh yesterday we heard what proved to be the last shells of the war, some of our own, or rather the Italian 12-inch howitzers going over on to M. Miatta. From now onwards it was downhill to the Brenta valley. At one point we passed a large ammunition dump which the Austrians had set on fire. It was exploding pretty freely and sending up some fragments unpleasantly close. One nearly hit Feild. A little later the road divided and transport and infantry had to part. We, having mules, were counted, quite unnecessarily as it turned out, as transport, and consequently took three hours longer to get in than the others did. We had to come down a tremendous precipice by means of a very long winding road, which at times was tunnelled. The views were magnificent. At last we came in sight of the lights of Caldonazza, which the men hailed with cheers, saying we had come to London. We got in there at 7.10 p.m. after 15 hours march, and then, to my fury, had no one to meet us and say where the billets were. I found some and put the men in, and then, while looking for brigade, ran across Feild, who showed me where the proper billets were, and so we moved in, joining up with the whole company in one big room. After we had settled in I was so overpoweringly sleepy that when Wigley gave me a cup of cocoa I put it down and went straight to sleep before I could drink it. So someone else did that for me.

Monday, 4th November.

We left at 9.30 a.m. The Colonel appeared for the first time since the show started, and proceeded to ask " Why that forage was left lying on the ground," and later, when we had stopped a few yards down the road, owing to a block in the traffic, " All drivers should dismount whenever the column halts." Not a word to the men or Feild as to how we had got on, or of praise for what they had done in the way of carrying, &c. Altogether to-day was pretty annoying, considering all things. Our next move, after parting with the Colonel, was to march four miles down a road before they discovered we were going the wrong way. We then turned about and marched back, going a round of an extra ten kilometres through Levico, along the side of a lake to Pergine, and then on to Vigalzano. Here we had civilian billets, and I had sheets, but no pyjamas. It was noticeable how many houses were able to produce an Italian flag when we marched through the towns.

Tuesday, 5th November.

An armistice came into force with Austria at 3 p.m. yesterday. So the war, as far as we are concerned, is finished. To-day and Wednesday we rested, doing little but clean up.

Thursday, 7th November.

At 10 a.m. we moved back through Pergine to Caldonazza, going the short way this time; and here we joined up again with the battalion, much to everyone's regret. We were billeted in an empty hotel. A show of this kind seems to demonstrate fairly clearly the superiority of the brigade company over the battalion organisation for M.G.'s. Even if they had wished to it was physically impossible for battalion headquarters to keep in touch with all four companies.

Friday, 8th November.

Webb rather peevish this morning. We started off again at 10 a.m. and marched up the hill by the short way. This was rather a tedious performance, as it was very steep indeed all the way. Every here and there the path was almost blocked by teleferica wires which had been cut down. We halted for an hour and had some cocoa, afterwards moving on to Vessena. Here we were billeted in an Austrian Corps ration dump, where we had excellent quarters, and so did the men. Close by there were sheds full of all kinds of good things. One contained some hundreds of tons of flour in large sacks, of which we took two or three, also a lot of soap, tea, stacks of potatoes, and tins of tomato soup. The room the sergeants used had a rather tinkly grand piano and a good deal of music, some Wagner and a large number of songs, including one of Hugo Wolf. I played for a little while, the first piano I had touched since coming to Italy. We had a very fine dinner, including some terrific 'armour piercing' dumplings with our stew, and plum duff. Rumours were current that Germany had given up.

Saturday, 9th November.

We left at 10 a.m. and marched down the Val d'Assa into Italy again. I rode part of the way, being in command of the company, as Feild was doing 'whipper in' at the back. We went quite easily down the hill to the Valle Portule and were put into various little huts all up the side of the valley. We got in at 4 p.m. Three men volunteered to go off with horses and fetch the typewriter from the top of Mosciagh, in case it was still there, and this they succeeded in doing, which was a rather fine piece of work. I slept alone in the mess rather uncomfortably as I had nothing but a coat on top of me and boards underneath.

Sunday, 10th November.

We left Portule at 8.30 a.m. and moved up hill along the side of the Val d'Assa, which was continually becoming steeper and narrower until we came to the edge of the spur, and down into Camporovere. It was curious to look across at the clearing and our other haunts on the opposite side of the plateau. We came through Asiago, already crowded with Italians, and even a few civilians, and then had a long struggle up through diamond north and east and Pria del Acqua to our old billets at Granessa,

which we were very lucky to get. We got in in time for lunch, and afterwards I took my section down to the baths, and had one myself, which was very necessary as well as refreshing. We thought we would like to go to the Curios, so Milner and I went up to book places, but were told it was for gunners only. I ran off to Division and saw Morshead. He put me on to someone else who arranged the whole thing, giving us fifty seats. We went at 8.30 p.m. and enjoyed ourselves very much.

Monday, 11th November.
Breakfast at 6.30 a.m. Off at 8.30 a.m. We went down the hills by a very steep mule track, I leading the company as before. We seemed to go a long way round and were pretty tired, but got to Thiene by 4.30 p.m. The men were all together in a large house : we all in the Officers' Club. Soon after we had arrived, Moss, the Adjutant, read out a telegram saying that Germany had signed an armistice agreement. Consequently we had a very good dinner. Afterwards someone lit a fire in the road opposite the Club, and helped it on with one or two petrol tins, and there was a good deal of jollification : officers were carried round the fire on the men's shoulders, and a band came and played. Still it was a trifle monotonous, and at 10.30 p.m. I went up to bed.

Tuesday, 12th November.
We moved at 9 a.m. to Brogliano, through Malo and up over the hills, again going a longer route than was necessary. This place is in the Agno valley and very pretty. We had the same billets the company were in when here last April : a silk factory some way outside the village, and quite separate from everyone else, which is a great point. I have a bed with sheets. Our mess is in a large stone paved room with an open fireplace. The only inhabitant of the house is a strange old woman, who trips about the room and laughs at us and talks unintelligibly.

Wednesday, 13th November—Saturday, 16th November.
We settled ourselves in and rested.

Sunday, 17th November.
Went to church in the afternoon and stayed for Communion afterwards. It was a thanksgiving service for the victory : we had the divisional band, which helped things on a bit. Major Feild went on leave, which makes me about third on the list.

Monday, 18th November.
We paraded in the morning ; that is, an hour's P.T. and football, an inspection, and limber cleaning. In the afternoon I played in a game of Rugger, officers against the rest. We won 6-0, after quite a good game.

From this point the war diary, as such, ceases. We remained for some months at Brogliano, waiting for demobilisation, and meanwhile going on English and Italian leave once or twice. To make an end I quote a rather flattering Order of the Day from our own (48th) Divisional Commander àpropos the recent operations.

ITALY

*Special Order of the Day
by Major-Gen. Sir H. B. Walker, K.C.B., D.S.O., Cmdg.
48th Division.*

Officers, N.C.O.'s, and Men of the 48th Division.

Your achievements during the last few days of the most profound military events deserve unstinted praise. After fourteen weeks of trench warfare and arduous work, chiefly at night, combined with raids of the most difficult though successful nature, you have undertaken an attack on a front originally allotted to two divisions against what ought to have been impregnable mountain positions ; you have swept away the enemy rearguards ; and acting as the vanguard of the 6th Italian Army you have advanced so rapidly and with such resolution that the enemy have had no time to reform and have left over 20,000 prisoners, hundreds of guns, and immeasureable booty in the hands of the Division.

The mere performance of the march in the time and under the conditions you endured, would have been, without opposition, considered a creditable feat. You can justly claim that the favourable situation of the Italian Armies on this front at 15.00 hours to-day, when one of the most memorable armistices in history was signed, is largely due to your exertions and resolution. As your Divisional General I cordially thank you.

4th November, 1918.

(Signed) H. B. WALKER, Maj.-Gen.,
Cmdg. 48th Div.

No. 4 Section, B Coy., 48th Bn., M.G.C.
October, 1918.

Section H.Q.
Sgt. H. R. Mole[1]   Sgt. W. J. Newman[2]
Pte. S. Wigley   Pte. G. Wortley (runner)

No. 13 team.   No. 14 team.
Cpl.   T. F. Taylor   Cpl.   W. Caton
L.-Cpl. W. Riley[3]   L.-Cpl. A. Paul
         F. J. Ferrell   W. Hodgkinson[1]
Pte.   H. Parminter   Pte.   R. Thompson
         G. Brown   McCulloch
         W. Perry   Appleby
         J. Gregson   J. Sweeting
         Blogg
         Currah

[1] Belgian Croix de Guerre.   [2] Military Medal and bar.   [3] Military Medal.

No. 15 team.   No. 16 team.
L.-Cpl. S. C. Farmar[1]   Cpl.   C. Sherwood
         A. B. Davies[2]   L.-Cpl. E. J. Noond
Pte.   H. T. Tutchings   Pte.   J. Imrie
         A. T. Chipperfield   E. A. Taylor
         C. Stockdale   J. Stock
         C. Sweeney   J. Brown
         Jameson[1]   H. Tustin
                                     Wright

Coy. Signallers.
         G. Horton   R. Howard
         H. James   J. Smart

[1] Died in hospital in Italy of influenza, Jan., 1919.   [2] Croce de Guerra, 10.ix.1918.

B Company, 2/8th Battalion, Worcestershire Regt.
21st January, 1918.

Officers.
Lt.   H. M. Adams, M.C.   A. Frost
2/Lt.   S. S. Jackson, M.C.   G. W. F. Grainger
        W. Rundle   V. Spencelagh
        G. A. Gale   J. Parker
        G. Radford

Coy. H.Q.
C.S.M.   Wilkes, C. J.   Pte. Pitt, T., cook
C.Q.M.S. George, R. F.   Moullé, F.   ,,
Cpl.   Stanley, A.   Wilkinson, J.
L.-Cpl. Saunders, A., Signals   Cooper, A. J.
Pte.   Hodges, R. W.   ,,   Hooper, R.
         Whittle, W.   ,,   Day, C., batman
         Gwilliam, H.   ,,   Cpl. King, F. W., D.C.M.,
         Johnson, G.   ,,   Lewis Guns.

	No. 5 Platoon.			No. 6 Platoon.
	Sgt. Smith, G.			Sgt. Westwood
	Pte. Chance, S.			Pte. White, E. A.
	Merriman, J.			Hanwell, H.
	Jeffcoat, G.			
No. 1 Sec.	Cpl. Andrews, E. J.	No. 4 Sec.	L.-Sgt. Dabbs, H. W.
	Pte. Moulder, H.		Pte. Dandy, E.
	Ballard, T.		Whinchurch, H. C.
	Smith, F. G.		Lea, W. A.
	Carwardine, G.		Heaps, P.
	Risch, T.		Vale, A.
	Rice, P. W.		Price, J.
	Cook, F. E.		Matthews, A.
No. 2 Sec.	L.-Cpl. Pratt, H. J.	No. 5 Sec.	L.-Cpl. Tandy, F.
	Pte. Drew, E.		Pte. Matheson, A.
	Male, T.		Evans, T. W.
	Mouland, J.		Weyman, W.
	Worth, W.		Woods, J. E.
	Yapp, J.		Bishop, F. W.
	Turpin, E.		Hill, J. F.
	Larcombe, W.		
No. 3 Sec.	L.-Cpl. Culverhouse	No. 6 Sec.	L.-Cpl. Stainer, E. H.
	Pte. Stevens		Pte. Suckling, T.
	Newey, C. W.		Nicholls, B.
	Grummitt, J.		Massey, N.
	Mullins, J.		Duckett, A.
	Powell, A.		Taylor, S.
	Seager, M. J.		Watson, T.
	Dawkins, H.		Johnson, W.
			Corbett, G.

	No. 7 Platoon.			No. 8 Platoon.
	Sgt. Portman			Sgt. Luxon
	L.-Sgt. Harris			Pte. Backhouse, A. E.
	Pte. Franklin, H. J.			Samways, W. G.
				Jones, E. C.
No. 7 Sec.	L.-Cpl. Hearn, F.	No. 10 Sec.	Cpl. Halford, J.
	Pte. Burns, W.		Pte. White, J.
	Davy, H.		Filer, F.
	Glenn, H.		Jones, G.
	Green, H. E.		Andrews, W. J.
	Harris, T.		Pawley, W.
	Lane, H.		Kirkham, J.
			Filer, H. M.
No. 8 Sec.	Cpl. Rudge, A.	No. 11 Sec.	L.-Cpl. Buley, P.
	Pte. Holland, P. W.		Pte. Ferriman, F.
	Allen, J. T.		Fenn, S.
	Chamberlain, A.		Holliday, A.
	Hodges, W. J.		Marsh, G. A.
	Lympany, C.		Jelfs, A.
	Brown, T.		Brommell, S.
			Stephenson, S.

No. 9 Sec.	L.-Cpl.	Wood, E.
	Pte.	Hodges, H. G.
		Armstrong, A.
		Coleman, F.
		Coombes, H.
		Rockwell, A.
		Stanley, W.
		Foster, C.
No. 12 Sec.	L.-Cpl.	Williams, S. G.
	Pte.	Brown, J. W.
		Andrews, J. F.
		Heritage, C.
		Chadbone, J.
		Jenkins, H. L.
		Jukes, W.
		Barker, F.
		Thompson, H.
		Cornwell, G.

INDEX

A

	Page
Abbeville	2
Ablaincourt	49
Acheux	40, 43, 45
Achicourt	65
Admiral's Rd.	76
Agnez-les-Duisans	67, 68
Agno	133
Ailly	48
Aire	2, 19
Aisne House	78
Albert	35-37, 40
Allen, Pte. G.	81
Ambrosini	112
Amiens	49, 51-52, 56, 58-9, 63, 86-7, 99, 106
Ancre R.	35, 36
Anderson, Lt.-Gen. Sir C. A.	25-6
Anderson, Major	91
d'Annunzio	119
Appleby, Pte.	127
Archer, Pte.	10
,, L.-Cpl.	17, 18, 26
Area 6	114, 130
Argenvillers	46, 48
Armentières	7, 10
Arquata	109, 110, 124
Arras	58, 64-6, 68, 84, 86, 89, 90, 92
Asiago	111, 118, 121, 129, 132
d'Assa, Val.	130, 132
Astico, R.	114-5
Atkins, I. A.	45
Attily	92, 104
Auchel	82
Australians, the	14
Authie, R.	33
Authuille	44
Auxi-le-Chateau	33
Ave	129
Aveluy	36-7, 40, 43, 80
Avesnes	65

B

	Page
Bach, J. S.	59
Bache, Cpl.	75
Bacquerot, Rue	7
Bailleul-aux-Cornailles	32, 34
Ball, Capt. A. E.	22, 53
Ball, Lt. R. A.	3, 6-9, 12

	Page
Baluchi Rd.	21, 23, 26
Bank Farm	77-9
Bapaume	87, 93
Baron, Major J.	120, 124, 126, 128
Bartleet, Major A. D.	24
Battcock, Major G. A.	129
Bavinchove	84
Bayonvillers	100
Beach, Pte.	18
Beaumont Hamel	35
Beauquesne	46
Beaurains	65
Beauval	63
Beauvois	105
Bedlam Buildings	8
Beethoven, L. v. B.	45
Beevor, Lt. J. K.	106
Berguette	2, 84
Berkeley Hotel	101
Berks Bn., 2/4th	97
,, 1/4th	129, 130
Bernaville	46
Bernheim, Lt.	22, 50
Bethencourt	55, 101
Bethune	25
Deuttler, Lt. (R.N.)	55
Bevan, Capt. J. H.	36, 91
Biddick, Cpl.	117
Bigwood, Capt. M. S.	8, 21, 29
Bilton, Lt.-Col. L. L.	12, 55, 71, 75, 79, 83, 86, 90, 10c
Bingham, Brig.-Gen. H.	53
Blackburne, Lt. G. M. I.	40
Blackmore, Lt. E.	121, 127-8
Blangermont	66, 71
Blauzce	110
Bois des Roses	61, 102
Bomford, Capt. D.	42
Bomford, Capt. J. F.	5, 30, 40, 42-3
Bomford, Lt. J. L.	5
Bond St.	29, 31
Bonnières	33
Bonvalot, Lt. A. C.	58-9
Booker, Lt. H.	29
Bosco	130
Boucher, Lt. B. E. C.	109, 110, 115
Boulogne	2, 41, 43, 67-8, 88-9, 106-7
Bouzincourt	35
Bowater, Pte.	14, 18
,, Cpl.	78-80, 83
Bowen, Pte.	81

139

INDEX

	Page
Bowyer, Capt. G. W.	64, 70-1
Bradford, Lt. K. J. G.	74
Brahms, Johannes	9, 18, 22, 34
Brandhoek	81
Bray-sur-Somme	98
Brenta	123
Brent-Smith, A. E.	45
Brentwood	18, 25, 105
Bright, Capt. B. H.	120
Britton, Pte.	18
Brogliano	133
Brooks, Major J. H.	124
Brown Line, the	60, 102-3
Brown, Lt.	64
Bruford, Pte.	62, 77-8
Brunialti	112-3, 116
Bucks Bn., 2/4th	77, 104
„ 1/4th	130
Bulford	3
Burford, Pte.	2
Busnes	32
Bussus-Bussue	48-9
Butcher, Capt. A. H.	10
Bute St.	30
Butler, Lt. M. K.	32-3, 63-4, 67, 69

C

	Page
Cade, Lt. F.	31
Caix	51
Calais	2, 42
Calderari, Lt.	124
Caldonazza	131-2
Call Farm	76
Call Reserve Trench	75
Cam Valley	92
Cambrai	51, 65, 92, 101
Cambrin	20
Camerons, 1st	89
Camiers	107-8
Campiello	110
Camporovere	130, 132
Canal Bank	82
Canaples	34
Candas	40, 43, 46
Canove	112, 121
Ca Paiella	117
Capitello Mulche	129
Capricorn Keep	77
Capricorn Trench	75-6
Carrépuits	100
Carriola	120
Casa del Guardiano	113
Cassel	83-4
Caswell, Lt. F. W.	81
Catz, M.	121, 130
Caulaincourt	56
Cenis, M.	109
Cepy Farm	61-2
Cesuna	114, 116, 120
Chambery	109
Chaplin, Chas.	126

	Page
Charlie Support Trench	85, 92
Chateau Road Trench	5, 21, 28
Chaulnes	54, 58, 106
Checkitts, Lt.-Col. F.	12
Chemical Trench	87
Cherry, A. C.	102-3
Cheshires, 15th Bn.	4-6, 51-2
„ 16th Bn.	58-9
Child, Sgt.	23
Chili Avenue	86, 92
Chopin, F.	22, 119
Chudleigh, Cpl.	24, 39, 82
Church Rd. tr.	28, 30-1
Churchill, Major	99
Cima d'Asta	123
Clarke, Lt. E. G.	18-22, 24, 32, 60-1
Clarke, Lt.-Col. R. J.	111, 120
Clegg, Lt. W.	87
Cliff, Capt. A.	3, 7
Coates, Lt. C.	39, 40, 44-5
Coates, Lt. T.	29, 67-8, 91
Coates, Lt.-Col.	95-6
Cockshy House	22
Cole, Lt. H. P.	44
Connaught, Duke of	88
Constable, Lt. O. C.	12, 15, 30-1, 86, 91, 96-8, 101
Copse St.	20
Corbie	52
Corelli	3
Corfu Avenue	87-8, 90
Corner Work	95-6
Cornet Malo	82
Corona Trench	87-9
Corps, IV.	51, 59
„ VI.	64-5
„ XVII.	86
„ XIX.	79
Costa Alley	92
Couchman, Lt. A. W.	110, 114, 124
Cox-Walker, Lt. J.	23
Crawley, Major, the Rev.	126
Crecy	46
Crick, Lt.	35
Crisp, Cpl.	117
Croix Barbée	4, 7-8
Croix Molignaux	55-6
Crowe, Lt. A. A.	55-6
Crucifix Corner	44
Cry Trench	85
Cunico	112
Cunningham, Lt. C. E.	4, 52
Cupid Trench	90
Curios, the	126-8, 133

D

	Page
Dainville	64, 95
Daniels, Sgt.	39
Davies, Major H. W.	74, 82, 98, 100-1, 104, 106
Day, Pte.	101
Death Valley (see Ravine, the)	38-9

INDEX

141

	Page
Dill, Capt. A. V.	11
Division IV.	91
" VII.	115, 123
" VIII.	52
" IX.	108
" XI.	43, 45
" XII.	86
" XV.	86, 92
" XVII.	84
" XXXV.	84
" XLVIII.	110-1, 134
" LVI.	70, 82
Dixon, Lt.	125
Domart-en-Ponthieu	34
Domart-St. Leger	34
Donovan, Pte.	81
Dorman, Lt.-Col.	61, 77-80
Doullens	33-4, 63-4, 71, 85
Dreslincourt	54
Drummond, Maj.-Gen. L. G.	18
Drury Lane	11, 12
Duck s Bill	6, 21, 24
Duddle, Lt.	72, 76
Duds, the	84
Durkin, Lt. F. V.	18, 20
Dutton, Lt. W. J.	110, 121

E

Early-Smith, Lt. J.	107
Edelweiss Spur	121
Edge, Lt. W.	4, 57, 62, 70, 79, 85, 90
Egypt	82
Elgar, Sir E.	100
Elliot, Sgt.	62
Englebelmer	36, 43
Epping	25
Equancourt	97-8, 100
Estaires	15, 17-19, 22-3, 27, 29-30
Etaples	2, 43, 107-8
Etrun	84
Euston Post.	5, 7, 28
Evers, Capt. H. L. 5, 9, 11, 30, 45, 48, 54, 65, 70, 72-4, 76. 80-1	
Eves, Cpl.	28, 81

F

Fampoux	87, 90, 92
Fara	118
Farmar, L.-Cpl.	120
Farm Ravine	96
Fauquissart	25
Fayet	61-2, 103-4
Feild, Capt. A. L.	111-end passim
Fenn, Capt. the Rev.	19
Fergusson, Lt.-Gen. Sir C.	87
Ffooks, Capt. W. A.	105
Field, Lt. H. H.	93-105 passim
Figwood	104
Filer, Pte.	102

	Page
Fillièvres	68-9
Fisher-Rowe, Lt.-Col. L.	16, 18, 29
Fisher-Rowe, Capt.	58
Fison, Capt. J. F. L.	51, 58
Flers	60
Folkestone	41-2, 67-8, 107
Follies, the	91
Fontinette	42-3
Foreste	101, 105-6
Fourques	58
Foweraker, Capt. T. S.	31, 72, 75, 82, 89-92
Fox, Lt. G. D. A.	16, 26
Framerville	49, 50, 52, 54
Francilly	102
Franck, César	18, 59
Franklin, Capt. A. F.	90-1, 105, 106
Franklin, Lt.	3, 6, 7
Fransu	34
Fresnoy-le-Petit	57, 105
Frevent	33, 68, 71
Fricker, Lt. E. G.	113-4, 126, 128
Frohen-le-Grand	33-4
Frohen-le-Petit	36
Frolics, the	86
Fryer, Capt. R. G.	103
Fulford, C. H.	51
Fuller Maitland, J. A.	32

G

Gale, Lt. G. A.	90, 100
Gallipoli	78
Gapennes	46
Garda, Ile de	110
Garda, Lake	119
Gardone	119
Gascoigne, Lt. B. B.	10, 16, 17
Genoa	109
Germaine	59, 60, 62, 101
Ghelpac	121
Givenchy-le-Noble	65
Gloucester Regt.—	
2/4th Bn., 6, 10, 14-16, 31-2, 40, 55, 60, 72, 75-76, 78, 88, 95	
1/4th Bn.	119, 121
2/6th Bn.	10, 18, 24, 45, 60
14th Bn.	5
Godbert, the	48, 52, 58-9, 86-7, 99, 106
Goldfish Chateau	74, 76, 83
Grandcourt	35-6, 39
Granezza	118, 120, 121, 124, 132
Grantham	105, 107, 111
Gravenstafel Rd.	75-6
Green, Lt.	111, 128
Green, Pte. F.	9
Green, J. R.	44
Grenadier Guards	58, 95
Griffiths, Major H. M.	3, 8, 30
Grosvenor Hotel	42, 68, 89
Guest, Cpl.	26, 81
Guest, Pte. S.	80-1

INDEX

H

	Page
Hackett, Pte.	18
Hainsselin, Lt.	98
Haking, Lt.-Gen. R. C. B.	3
Halford, Pte. J.	5, 102
Hamilton, Lt.	115
,, Cpl.	117, 120, 122, 126
,, Pte.	126
Hannay, Major J. R.	93
Hansa Line	45
Harbonnieres	51
Hart Copse	54
Havre	1
Havrincourt Wood	93
Hawkins, Capt.	51
Hayes, Lt.	11, 17
Hazard St.	20
Heaphy, Lt. W.	111, 114
Heathcock, Lt. D. W.	107-8, 110-1, 115, 117, 125, 126
Hedauville	40, 45-6
Hellencourt Farm	46
Henry VIII.	107
Herleville	49, 53, 63
Hervey, Lt. G. A. K.	25
Hesdin	60
Hewson, Lt. J.	111-2, 114-6
Heywood, Capt.	88
High Trench	38
Hilloek	83
Hindenburg Line	51, 93-4, 96
Hinges	4
Hingley, L.-Cpl.	26
Holcroft, Capt. C. W.	80, 91, 94-6, 98, 101, 103
Holcroft, Lt. H. R.	79, 82, 92
Holnon	60-2, 104
Honeysett, Pte.	80-1
Hopkins, Capt. G. W.	44
Horton, Sig.	129
Hotel d'Amiens	68
,, Belfort	87, 90
,, de Commerce	91, 92
,, Folkestone	88-9, 106
,, de France	33, 68, 71
,, Genoa	109
,, du Louvre	107
,, Luna	111, 119-20
,, Meurice	68
,, Regie Terme	119
,, du Rhin	50
,, Westminster	108
Hughes, Pte.	18, 78, 80
Hugman, Capt.	127-8
Huit Maisons	19
Huitres, les	51-2, 58-9, 86
Hun St.	20, 27-9
Hunt, L.-Cpl.	18, 20
,, Lt.	108
,, Pte. J.	105
Hunter Weston, Lt.-Gen.	73
Husb Hall	21-2, 26-7

I

	Page
Impey, Cpl.	100
Inns of Court O.T.C.	93, 106
Interlaken	119

J

Jackson, Lt.	96-7, 99, 100-1
Jocks, the	87
Jones, Pte.	102
Jupiter	30

K

Kaberlaba	125, 128
Kansas Cross	73
Keble College	16, 58
Keeper's House	57, 106
King, Lt.	11, 17
,, Cpl. F. W.	95, 100
King's Manor, the	107
King's Regt., the	97-8, 89
Kippon, Lt.	74
Knight, Cpl.	6-7
Kratz Wood	53, 55

L

La Bassée Rd.	5, 7, 20, 24, 26-7, 30
La Fosse	4, 5, 8, 9, 29, 30
La Gorgue	9, 10, 15, 16, 18, 21-6, 28-9
Langley, H. F. G.	3, 51
La Vacquerie	93, 95, 100
Laventie	10, 12, 13, 15, 16, 17, 22, 27, 33, 40, 60
La Vicogne	54-5
Lawe R.	8
Leck, Capt. D. H.	71, 74, 102-3
Lekeu	58
Le Meillard	46
Le Mesurier, Capt. H.	4
Lens	66
Le Quesnel	35-4
Lestrem	8
Le Touquet	91
Levico	131
Ligny-St. Flochel	35
Lihons	51
Lille	128
Lillers	32
Linzeux	68-9
Liszt	26, 119
Lodoletta	110
Lomax, Lt.-Col.	124
London	131
Long, Major B.	125-6
Loom of Youth	124
Loretto Post	5, 8
Loupart Wood	96

INDEX

	Page
Lovell, Lt.	108
Lucas, L.-Cpl.	4
Lyautey, P. C.	55

M

	Page
Macaulay, Lord	106
Mackenzie, Maj.-Gen. C.	19, 23, 29, 32, 60, 68, 73, 97, 102
Magna Boschi	114
Maissemy	104, 105
Maldon	18, 59
Malo	116
Manancourt	98
Manchester Hill	102-3
Manchester Regt., 5th Bn.	81, 105
Manuel, Lt. A.	11
Marcelcave	49, 100
Mare	117
Marginal Line	114, 120, 123, 126-7
Marindin, Lt.-Col.	26
Marlborough College	12, 16, 25, 44, 98, 124
Marteville	57, 105
Martin, 2/Lt.	95
Martinsart	35, 44-5, 49
Mascagni	110
Mass in D	125
Masselot St.	17
Massey, Pte.	18
Mauquissart	21
Maxwell, Lt.	52
Medland, Cpl.	26, 30, 81
Mendelssohn	26
Mennie, Lt. J. B.	58-9
Mentières	90
Merancourt	57
Merville	19, 24, 20, 29
Mesnil	35-6
Metz	93, 97
Miatta M.	131
Mignet	48
Milan	110
Miller, Capt. G. C.	76
Milliner, Cpl.	30
Milner, Lt. S. A.	111-end passim
Mitchell, Capt. E. S.	90-1, 94, 97, 104-6
Mitchelmore, Cpl.	24, 28, 87
Moated Grange	10
Modane	100
Mogg's Hole	23, 30-1
Monchy Lagache	56-7
Monchy Le Preux	65
Monte Carlo	104
Montigny	34
Moreuil	52
Morgan, Capt. S. F.	4
Morris, Lt.	68-70, 85
Morshead, Capt. O. F.	45, 46
„ Major	116, 124, 133
Mortimer, Capt. A. E.	50, 62-3, 74, 100
Mosciegh, M.	130-2
Moss, Capt.	133
Mouquet Farm	36-7, 40, 44, 49
Mullet, Lt. W. G.	44, 70
Munro, Gen. Sir C.	8
Myers, Cpl.	39

N

	Page
Nab Rd.	36-7, 40
Naish, Sgt.	130
Nameless House	120
Neb, the	28
Nesle	55, 58-9, 63, 101
Neuve Chappelle	3, 4, 10, 13, 16, 21-2, 26, 32
Newman, Sgt.	112, 130
Nieppe, Forêt de	19
Noond, Cpl.	129
Norwood, Pte.	81
"Notts and Derbys"	8

O

	Page
Ococches	33
Odgers, Capt. W. A.	11, 30
"Old Gent." (see Walford, Capt.)	
Orchard Trench	20
Orlencourt	32
Ostend	128
Ovillers	37
Oxford St.	31

P

	Page
Paradis	29, 32
Paradis, Rue de	22
Paris	106, 108
Parker, 2/Lt.	103
Parry-Jones, Capt. M. M.	10, 70-1, 82
Parsons, Lt. B. K.	44
Parsons, Cpl.	61-3, 78-9
Partut	112
de la Pasture, Mrs.	25
Peach, Capt.	52
Perghele	113
Pergine	131-2
Perham Down	1
Perry, Lt. P. P.	38, 71, 90, 96
Pertain	54
Peschiere	119-20
Petit Houvin	71
Picantin	13, 15, 16
Pilkington, Capt.	100
Plateau Station	98
Pommern	77, 79
Pond Farm	76, 80
Pont du Hem	26
Pont Remy	49
Poole, Lt.	81
Poperinghe	74, 76, 81-3
Port Arthur	21
Portule, val.	130, 132

144 INDEX

	Page
Potte	55
Poupée, La	74, 81, 83
Press, Lt. A. H.	26, 30, 118, 122-4, 127, 130
Priabona	116
Pria del acqua	132
Price, Pte.	110
Pritchard, Lt. C. H.	25
Prouville	34, 40

Q

Quatre Fils Gaymon	64, 71
Queen, the	69
Queen Hotel	42
Quesnel	52

R

Rabone, Lt. E. S.	3, 7, 39
,, Capt.	67, 70, 82
Ravine, the	38-9
Rawlings, Lt.	106
Rawlinson, Gen. Sir H.	52
Raymond, Lt.	50
Read, Lt.	121
Red House	13
Red lamp corner	32
Regina Trench	38-9, 50
Ribeaucourt	34
Richards, Lt.	85, 104
Richebourg (St. Vaast)	5, 27, 29, 42
Riez Bailleul	6-7
Rifle Dump	33
Rifleman's Avenue	13-14
Robecq	2
Rocourt	103
Rodighieri	121, 129
Rolfe, Lt.	58
Romescamps	108
Rose, Lt.	56
Rosières	52
Rotten Row	12, 16
Rouge Croix	26
Rouvroy	03
Rowe, Capt. A. V.	2, 3, 7, 70
Roye	100
Rua	115
Rubrouck	73
Rue du Bois	20
Ruffer, H.	50
Rugby	98
Rumpelmayer's	108-9
Rundle, Lt.	101-3
Ruyaulcourt	93

S

Sadler, Lt.	71, 87
Sage, Lt.	10, 15-23
Salo	119
Salonika	105
Sarcedo	117
Saunders, Pte.	78
Savoy Hotel	107
Savy	102-3
Scadding, Pte.	78
Scarpe, R.	86
Schuler Galleries	78
Scrivia, R.	100
Sec	127, 129
Second Assembly Trench	30
Selby, Pte.	48
Selency	102, 104
Senlis	35
Serpentine Trench	40, 50
Sherborne	10
Sherwood, Cpl.	129
Shinn, Dr.	25
Sign Post Lane	21
Simencourt	66, 84
Singleton, Lt.-Col.	91
Sirmione	119
Skerratt, Pte.	18
Skey, Lt.	45-47
Skindles	74
Sleap, Lt. J. W.	56-7
Smith, Lt.	24, 60, 96
Solent, the	1
Somme Farm	77-8, 80
Somme R.	29, 35, 49, 55, 101
Southampton	1
Spades, the	86
Spooner, Brig.-Gen.	50, 53, 70, 97, 105
Sproule, Lt. W.	126
S. Sisto	118, 120-2, 124, 129
St. Acheul	34
St. Eloi	86
St. Jean	75-6
St. Nicholas' camp	81, 86
St. Omer	2
St. Pol	32-3, 47, 69, 70-1
St. Quentin	60-1, 102-3, 114
St. Quentin Wood	57
St. Riquier	48
St. Venant	3, 9, 10, 18-9
Stafford, Lt.	110, 118
Stallard, Capt. R.	74, 92-4
Stanley, Capt.	43, 46, 70
Steenbecque	19
Steenbecque R. (Ypres)	76-7, 79
Stella	112
Stevenson, Capt. R. W.	53, 89
Stevenson, Lt.	59, 60
Stockwell, Brig.-Gen.	73
Stone, Lt. H. C.	77
Stone, Lt. J. A.	110, 121
Strand	11
Sugar loaf, the	16
Sus-St. Leger	64
Sutherland, Av.	13, 14
Symons, Lt. N. V. H.	1, 4, 5, 9, 15, 18, 105

Page

T

Talbot, Rev. N. - 46
Tanner, Lt. L. E. - 19
Tarrant, C. S. M. - 95
Taylor, Cpl. - 113
Taylor, Pte. - 78
Ternas - 33
Tescia - 112
Tête de Boeuf - 48
Tetlow, Lt. K. B. - 79, 80, 97
Tezze - 116, 124
Thacker, Capt. N. - 10-106 passim
Thiene - 110-1, 116-7, 119-20, 124, 133
Thiepval - 34-5
Thomlinson, Lt. F. B. - 26, 30, 52, 61, 71
Thompson, Capt. - 106
Tiddy, Lt. R. J. E. - 18
Tidworth - 1, 8, 97
Tilleloy, Rue - 13, 16, 17
Tilleloy, South - 6, 7
Tilloy-les-Mofflaines - 65
Trefcon - 56
Trin. Coll. Cambs. - 98
Trissino - 124
Troutbeck, Lt. J. M. - 3
Tulloch Corner - 37, 44, 56, 70
Turin - 109
Tustin, Pte. - 123
Tutchings, Pte. - 129

U

Uhlan Farm - 75, 78

V

Vachell, H. A. - 21
Vacher, Lt. W. E. - 10-99 passim
Varennes - 46
Vauban - 91
Vauvillers - 50
Vaux - 101
Vaux-en-Amienois - 51-2, 58-9
Venice - 110, 115
Venus - 76
Vermand - 99, 100
Vermandovillers - 49, 50, 52
Vessena - 131-2
Vicenza - 110, 119, 120
Victoria - 41-2, 67, 106-7, 125
Vigalzano - 131
Villers Bretonneux - 52, 99, 106
Villers Bocage - 93, 100
Villers Pluich - 93, 96-7
Villevecque - 56, 104
Vlamertinghe - 75

W

Wagner, R. - 132
Wailly - 65
Wainwright, Capt. the Rev. R. C. - 97
Wake, Lt.-Col. H. - 15, 91
Walford, Capt. J. O. - 11, 19, 30, 74, 122
Walker, Maj.-Gen. H. B. - 125, 133-4
Wall, Lt. - 107-111
Wallace, Lt. - 80
Walters, Cpl. - 28, 60
Warburton, Capt. - 68
Ward, Mrs. Wilfrid - 110
Wardrop, Lt. E. G. 21, 22, 57, 60, 74, 90, 93
Warloy - 35
Warlus - 67
Warner, Cpl. - 117
Warwicks, 5th Bn. - 94-5
Wavans - 33-4
Weare, Pte. - 78, 80
Webb, Capt. G. A. 111, 116, 118, 121, 125, 132
Webb, Cpl. - 120
Weeks, Pte.
8-9, 22, 38-9, 44, 50, 54, 58, 60, 67, 70, 72, 81-2, 90, 97, 105-6
Weyman, Pte. - 97, 101
Wheeler, Pte. - 12
White, Pte. (L.T.M.B.) - 18
White, Pte. (8th Worcs.) - 102
Wick Salient - 16
Widdows, Lt. F. M. - 82
Wieltje - 74, 77, 79, 81-2
Wiencourt - 49
Wigley, Pte. - 116, 121-2, 130-1
Williams, Sgt. - 72, 87
Williams, Cpl. - 103
Williamson, C. N. and A. M. - 23
Winchester Post - 24
Winchester Trench - 21, 24
Wine House - 76
Winnepeg - 73
Wolf, Hugo - 133
Worcesters—
1st Bn. - 58
2/7th Bn. 8, 10, 15, 19, 25, 28-9, 34, 40, 61, 71, 77, 80, 90, 92, 102-3, 105-6
1/8th Bn. - 122
2/8 Bn. 23, 30-1, 45, 54, 59, 65, 69, 70, 74, 79, 82, 85, 122
Wright, Capt. - 114
Wright, Pte. - 81
Wurst Farm - 75
Wyatt, Capt. - 16, 64
,, Major - 95

Y

Y - 50
Ypres - 3, 73-5, 81, 86, 89, 97

Z

Zeggers Cappel - 72, 74
Zigzag - 79
Zollern Trench - 38, 40

www.ingramcontent.com/pod-product-compliance
Lightning Source LLC
Chambersburg PA
CBHW011328190426

43193CB00047B/2923